STRATEGIES
TO
ACHIEVE
MATHEMATICS
SUCCESS

STAMS™ Series

BOOK

6

W9-BJN-763

CURRICULUM ASSOCIATES®, Inc.

ISBN 0-7609-1174-6

©2001—Curriculum Associates, Inc.

North Billerica, MA 01862

15 14 13 12 11 10 9 8 7 6 5 4 3

TABLE OF CONTENTS

Strategy One BUILDING NUMBER SENSE

Study the place-value chart that Kim's math teacher made for a sixth-grade bulletin-board display. As you study, note the placement of commas. Also note the digits to the right of the decimal. Consider how commas and decimals help you understand the value of digits in numbers.

hundred millions (100,000,000)	ten millions (10,000,000)	millions (1,000,000)	hundred thousands (100,000)	ten thousands (10,000)	thousands (1,000)	hundreds (100)	tens (10)	ones (1)	tenths (0.1)	hundredths (0.01)
1	6	8,	5	7	3,	4	0	9	.2	3

The number 168,573,409.23 is written as one hundred sixty-eight million, five hundred seventy-three thousand, four hundred nine, and twenty-three hundredths. When writing a number with a decimal, the word *and* takes the place of the decimal.

The number can be shown as 100,000,000 + 60,000,000 + 8,000,000 + 500,000 + 70,000 + 3,000 + 400 + 9 + $\frac{23}{100}$.

Look at some other numbers and how they can be written.

The number 43,000 = 43 thousands = 430 hundreds = 4,300 tens. The number 43,000 can also be written as $4(10^4) + 3(10^3)$ or as $4.3(10^4)$.

The number 38,000,000,000 = 38 billions = 38,000 millions. The number 38,000,000,000 can also be written as $3(10^{10}) + 8(10^9)$ and as 3.8×10^{10}.

You use **number sense** when you think about the place value of each digit in a number.

▶ Each digit in a number has a place value, such as ones, tens, hundreds, or thousands. The value of a digit depends on its place in the number.

▶ A comma separates groups of three digits in large numbers. Look at the placement of any commas when trying to determine the value of digits in large numbers.

▶ In a number with a decimal, a digit that is one place to the right of the decimal is in the tenths place. A digit that is two places to the right of the decimal is in the hundredths place. The value of a number in the tenths place is greater than the value of a number in the hundredths place.

▶ A number may be written in digits or in words.

Kim made her own place-value chart. Study the number that Kim wrote in her chart. Think about each digit and its place value. Then do Numbers 1 through 4.

hundred millions (100,000,000)	ten millions (10,000,000)	millions (1,000,000)	hundred thousands (100,000)	ten thousands (10,000)	thousands (1,000)	hundreds (100)	tens (10)	ones (1)	tenths (0.1)	hundredths (0.01)
4	2	9,	3	1	7,	1	8	0	.5	6

1. What is the place value of the 4 in Kim's number?

Ⓐ 4 millions

Ⓑ 40 millions

Ⓒ 400 millions

Ⓓ 4 hundred thousands

2. What is the value of the 5 in Kim's number?

Ⓐ 5

Ⓑ 0.5

Ⓒ 0.05

Ⓓ 50

3. What is the place value of the 6 in Kim's number?

Ⓐ 6 tens

Ⓑ 6 tenths

Ⓒ 6 hundreds

Ⓓ 6 hundredths

4. Which of these is equal to the value of the 9 in Kim's number?

Ⓐ 9×10^7

Ⓑ 9×10^6

Ⓒ $9 \times 100,000$

Ⓓ 9×10^8

Talk about your answers to questions 1–4. Tell why you chose the answers you did.

Remember: You use number sense when you think about the place value of each digit in a number.

▶ Each digit in a number has a place value, such as ones, tens, hundreds, or thousands. The value of a digit depends on its place in the number.

▶ A comma separates groups of three digits in large numbers. Look at the placement of any commas when trying to determine the value of digits in large numbers.

▶ In a number with a decimal, a digit that is one place to the right of the decimal is in the tenths place. A digit that is two places to the right of the decimal is in the hundredths place. The value of a number in the tenths place is greater than the value of a number in the hundredths place.

▶ A number may be written in digits or in words.

Solve this problem. As you work, ask yourself, "What do any commas tell me about the value of a digit in a large number?"

5. Kim learned that the temperature at the core of the sun is 27,000,000°F. Which of these is equal to the value of the 27 in 27,000,000?

   Ⓐ 2.7×10^5

   Ⓑ 2.7×10^7

   Ⓒ 2.7×10^8

   Ⓓ 2.7×10^6

Solve another problem. As you work, ask yourself, "What does the position of a digit to the right of a decimal in a number tell me about its place value?"

6. Kim read that, in 1969, astronauts took 838.20 pounds of moon rocks back to Earth to study. What is the place value of the 2 in 838.20?

   Ⓐ 2 hundreds

   Ⓑ 2 hundredths

   Ⓒ 2 tenths

   Ⓓ 2 tens

**Look at the answer choices for each question.
Read why each answer choice is correct or not correct.**

5. Kim learned that the temperature at the core of the sun is 27,000,000°F. Which of these is equal to the value of the 27 in 27,000,000?

Ⓐ 2.7×10^5

This answer is not correct because it equals 2.7 × 100,000, or 270,000, but not 27,000,000.

● 2.7×10^7

This answer is correct because it equals 2.7 × 10,000,000, or 27,000,000.

Ⓒ 2.7×10^8

This answer is not correct because it equals 2.7 × 100,000,000, or 270,000,000, but not 27,000,000.

Ⓓ 2.7×10^6

This answer is not correct because it equals 2.7 × 1,000,000, or 2,700,000, but not 27,000,000.

6. Kim read that, in 1969, astronauts took 838.20 pounds of moon rocks back to Earth to study. What is the place value of the 2 in 838.20?

Ⓐ 2 hundreds

This answer is not correct because the 2 is in the tenths place, not in the hundreds place.

Ⓑ 2 hundredths

This answer is not correct because the 2 is in the tenths place, not in the hundredths place.

● 2 tenths

This answer is correct because the 2 is in the tenths place, one place to the right of the decimal.

Ⓓ 2 tens

This answer is not correct because the 2 is in the tenths place, not in the tens place.

You use number sense to understand fractions.

▶ In a fraction, the **numerator**, or top number, stands for one or more parts of the whole. The **denominator**, or bottom number, stands for all the parts of the whole.

▶ Fractions can be added and subtracted. To add or subtract fractions with different denominators, first find their least common denominator. The least common denominator of the fractions $\frac{2}{3}$ and $\frac{1}{4}$ is 12, because 12 is the lowest common multiple of 3 and 4.

Change	To	Add	Subtract
$\frac{2}{3}$ $\frac{1}{4}$	$\frac{8}{12}$ $\frac{3}{12}$	$\frac{8}{12} + \frac{3}{12} = \frac{11}{12}$	$\frac{8}{12} - \frac{3}{12} = \frac{5}{12}$

▶ Fractions can be multiplied. To find the product of fractions, multiply the numerator of each fraction; then multiply the denominators.

$\frac{3}{7} \times \frac{5}{11} = \frac{3 \times 5}{7 \times 11} = \frac{15}{77}$

▶ An improper fraction is equal to more than a whole. To convert an improper fraction to a mixed number, divide the numerator by the denominator.

$\frac{28}{8} = 28 \div 8 = 3\frac{1}{2}$

Kim's class is planning an international food fair. Do Numbers 7 through 10.

7. The students formed 8 groups. The shaded part of the figure shows how many groups will make food. What fraction of the groups will do other jobs?

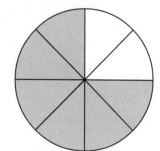

  Ⓐ $\frac{3}{4}$ Ⓒ $\frac{3}{8}$

  Ⓑ $\frac{1}{4}$ Ⓓ $\frac{5}{8}$

8. The fraction $\frac{30}{4}$ is equal to the number of cups of cheese needed for the enchiladas. How much cheese is needed?

  Ⓐ 6 cups   Ⓒ $7\frac{1}{4}$ cups

  Ⓑ $6\frac{1}{2}$ cups   Ⓓ $7\frac{1}{2}$ cups

9. A recipe for sukiyaki calls for $\frac{1}{3}$ cup soy sauce and $\frac{1}{2}$ cup beef broth. What is the sum of these two ingredients?

  Ⓐ $\frac{5}{6}$ cup

  Ⓑ $\frac{2}{5}$ cup

  Ⓒ $\frac{1}{5}$ cup

  Ⓓ $\frac{1}{6}$ cup

10. Kim wants to use only $\frac{1}{2}$ of $\frac{1}{3}$ cup soy sauce to make sukiyaki. What is $\frac{1}{2}$ of $\frac{1}{3}$ cup?

  Ⓐ $\frac{5}{6}$ cup

  Ⓑ $\frac{2}{5}$ cup

  Ⓒ $\frac{1}{6}$ cup

  Ⓓ $1\frac{1}{6}$ cups

Kim's uncle is a chef in an Italian restaurant. Read his recipe for pizza sauce. Then do Numbers 11 through 14.

Joe's Famous Pizza Sauce

$\frac{1}{4}$ cup chopped onion

1 teaspoon minced garlic

$1\frac{1}{2}$ tablespoons olive oil

$2\frac{1}{3}$ cups tomatoes, chopped in a blender

$\frac{3}{4}$ cup tomato paste

$1\frac{3}{4}$ teaspoons dried basil

$1\frac{1}{2}$ teaspoons dried oregano

$\frac{3}{4}$ teaspoon salt

$\frac{1}{8}$ teaspoon pepper

Cook onion and garlic in olive oil until tender. Add tomatoes, tomato paste, basil, oregano, salt, and pepper. Bring to a boil. Then cover and simmer for 40 minutes, or $\frac{2}{3}$ of an hour.

11. Kim plans to add $\frac{1}{3}$ cup onions to the $\frac{1}{4}$ cup in the recipe. What is the sum of $\frac{1}{3}$ cup and $\frac{1}{4}$ cup?

Ⓐ $\frac{3}{4}$ cup

Ⓑ $\frac{7}{12}$ cup

Ⓒ $\frac{1}{12}$ cup

Ⓓ $\frac{2}{7}$ cup

12. Kim wants to change the recipe and use $\frac{16}{3}$ cups tomatoes. Which of these is equal to $\frac{16}{3}$ cups?

Ⓐ $8\frac{1}{3}$ cups

Ⓑ 36 cups

Ⓒ $5\frac{1}{3}$ cups

Ⓓ $6\frac{2}{3}$ cups

13. Kim cooked the sauce for $\frac{2}{5}$ of the time shown in the recipe. What is $\frac{2}{5} \times \frac{2}{3}$ hour?

Ⓐ $\frac{1}{2}$ hour

Ⓑ $3\frac{3}{4}$ hours

Ⓒ $\frac{3}{10}$ hour

Ⓓ $\frac{4}{15}$ hour

14. The circle shows how many jars of pizza sauce Kim made. The shaded portion shows how many jars she gave away. What fraction shows the portion she kept?

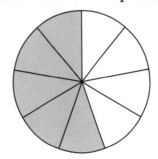

Ⓐ $\frac{5}{9}$ Ⓒ $\frac{4}{9}$

Ⓑ $\frac{1}{2}$ Ⓓ $\frac{1}{4}$

▶ A test question about number sense may ask for the value of a digit in a number.

▶ A test question about number sense may ask for a number in its different forms.

▶ A test question about number sense may ask the place value of a decimal.

▶ A test question about number sense may ask the sum or product of fractions or the expression of an improper fraction as a mixed number.

Read the information that Kim learned in a documentary film about the United States Postal Service. Then do Numbers 15 and 16.

Facts About the Mail

Kim discovered that each year, the United States Postal Service collects about 107 billion pieces of first-class mail from 312,000 collection boxes and thousands of businesses, schools, and other locations.

Building Number Sense

15. Kim learned that in one year the postal service employed 892,869 people to help deliver mail. Which of these represents the value of the 89 in 892,869?

Ⓐ 8.9×10^5

Ⓑ 8.9×10^6

Ⓒ 8.9×10^4

Ⓓ 8.9×10^7

Building Number Sense

16. Kim also found out that the U.S. handles about $\frac{2}{5}$ of the world's mail daily. Japan handles $\frac{3}{50}$ of the world's mail daily. What fraction shows the sum of $\frac{2}{5}$ and $\frac{3}{50}$?

Ⓐ $\frac{6}{55}$

Ⓑ $\frac{1}{11}$

Ⓒ $\frac{1}{25}$

Ⓓ $\frac{23}{50}$

Kim read a story about a boy who started a foundation called Children in Need.
Read what Kim did after she read the story. Then do Numbers 17 and 18.

Packaged Goods

After reading the story, Kim collected money, food, clothing, and books to send to the foundation. Kim and her friends packed the goods into boxes. After getting instructions from the foundation, Kim mailed the boxes to different places around the world.

Building Number Sense

17. One box of clothing that Kim sent to Nicaragua weighed 7.459 ounces. What is the place value of the 5 in 7.459?

Ⓐ 50

Ⓑ 5

Ⓒ 5 tenths

Ⓓ 5 hundredths

Building Number Sense

18. A group in Kim's town donates $\frac{3}{10}$ of its annual dues. This year, the group gave $\frac{1}{4}$ of their donation to Children in Need. What is $\frac{1}{4} \times \frac{3}{10}$?

Ⓐ $\frac{4}{14}$

Ⓑ $\frac{3}{4}$

Ⓒ $\frac{3}{40}$

Ⓓ $\frac{7}{40}$

Strategy Two USING ESTIMATION

PART ONE: Learn About Estimation

Study the numbers in the estimation chart that Jack made. Estimation is used to find a number that is close to an exact number. As you study, think about how to find an estimate.

Number	Nearest 10	Nearest 100	Nearest 1,000	Nearest 10,000	Nearest 100,000	Nearest 1,000,000
746,776	746,780	746,800	747,000	750,000	700,000	1,000,000
2,138,223	2,138,220	2,138,200	2,138,000	2,140,000	2,100,000	2,000,000
34,728,191	34,728,190	34,728,200	34,728,000	34,730,000	34,700,000	35,000,000

You use estimation to find the nearest ten, hundred, thousand, ten thousand, and so forth, of a number. You can also estimate to find the nearest whole number, nearest ten, and so forth, of a mixed number.

When estimating whole numbers, remember that 5 is the midpoint for rounding. Numbers less than 5 are rounded down. Numbers 5 and above are rounded up.

When estimating a mixed number, round up if the fraction is $\frac{1}{2}$ or more; round down if the fraction is less than $\frac{1}{2}$. The estimate for the mixed number is $72\frac{5}{7}$, to the nearest whole number, is 73.

You also use estimation to check if an answer to a math problem is reasonable.

For addition, round the addends. Their estimated sum will be close to the actual sum.

For multiplication, round the larger factor. Round factors that are mixed numbers.

$62 \times 9 \quad \rightarrow \quad 60 \times 9 = 540$

$15\frac{1}{2} \times 45 \quad \rightarrow \quad 16 \times 50 = 800$

$22\frac{1}{8} \times 37\frac{3}{5} \quad \rightarrow \quad 22 \times 38 = 836$

$182 \times 20 \quad \rightarrow \quad 200 \times 20 = 4,000$

You use **estimation** to find a number that is close to another number. You also use estimation to check if a sum or product is reasonable.

▶ Numbers can be rounded to the nearest ten, hundred, thousand, ten thousand, and so forth.

▶ To round a mixed number, find its nearest whole number or its nearest ten.

Jack wrote a report about Singapore. Read this part of Jack's report. As you read, think about strategies for finding estimates. Then do Numbers 1 through 4.

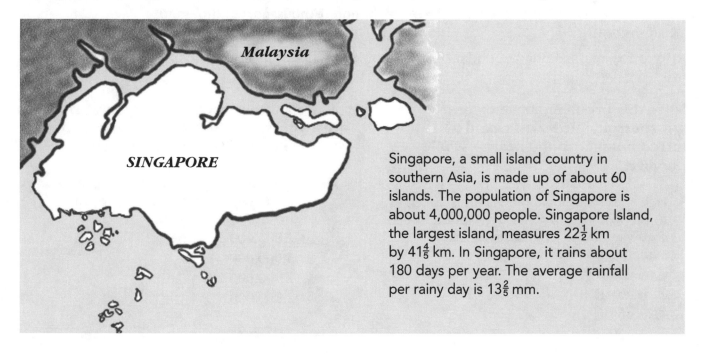

Singapore, a small island country in southern Asia, is made up of about 60 islands. The population of Singapore is about 4,000,000 people. Singapore Island, the largest island, measures $22\frac{1}{2}$ km by $41\frac{4}{5}$ km. In Singapore, it rains about 180 days per year. The average rainfall per rainy day is $13\frac{2}{5}$ mm.

1. To the nearest whole number, about how many millimeters of rain fall on a rainy day?
   Ⓐ 12 mm
   Ⓑ 13 mm
   Ⓒ 14 mm
   Ⓓ 10 mm

2. Jack wanted to figure about how much rainfall Singapore gets in 10 rainy days. What was his correct estimate?
   Ⓐ 130 mm
   Ⓑ 100 mm
   Ⓒ 140 mm
   Ⓓ 125 mm

3. Jack had rounded the population of Singapore to 4,000,000. Which of the following could be the actual population?
   Ⓐ 4,600,000
   Ⓑ 3,400,150
   Ⓒ 4,821,720
   Ⓓ 3,531,600

4. Jack wanted to estimate the area of Singapore Island, which is roughly rectangular. He estimated, to the nearest whole number, the width and length of the island. What was his correct estimate?
   Ⓐ 800 square km
   Ⓑ 902 square km
   Ⓒ 966 square km
   Ⓓ 1,000 square km

Work with a partner.

Talk about your answers to questions 1–4. Tell why you chose the answers you did.

Remember: You use estimation to find a number that is close to another number. You can also use estimation to check if a sum or product is reasonable.

▶ Numbers can be rounded to the nearest ten, hundred, thousand, ten thousand, and so forth.

▶ To round a mixed number, find its nearest whole number or its nearest ten.

Solve this problem. As you work, ask yourself, "How do I round a mixed number to the nearest whole number?"

5. Jack read that Singapore Island is linked to the mainland by a $3,464\frac{7}{10}$-foot raised roadway. To the nearest foot, what is the length of this roadway?

Ⓐ 3,467 ft

Ⓑ 3,464 ft

Ⓒ 3,465 ft

Ⓓ 3,460 ft

Solve another problem. As you work, ask yourself, "How do I round a number to the nearest hundred thousand?"

6. The population of the city of Singapore is 2,812,000. What number is closest to the city's population?

Ⓐ 2,800,000

Ⓑ 3,000,000

Ⓒ 2,900,000

Ⓓ 2,850,000

Look at the answer choices for each question.
Read why each answer choice is correct or not correct.

5. Jack read that Singapore Island is linked to the mainland by a $3,464\frac{7}{10}$-foot raised roadway. To the nearest foot, what is the length of this roadway?

Ⓐ 3,467 ft

This answer is not correct because $\frac{7}{10}$ is more than $\frac{1}{2}$ and therefore rounds up to 1: 3,464 + 1 = 3,465, not 3,467.

Ⓑ 3,464 ft

This answer is not correct because $\frac{7}{10}$ is more than $\frac{1}{2}$ and therefore rounds up to 1: 3,464 + 1 = 3,465, not 3,464.

● 3,465 ft

This answer is correct because $\frac{7}{10}$ is more than $\frac{1}{2}$ and therefore rounds up to 1: 3,464 + 1 = 3,465.

Ⓓ 3,460 ft

This answer is not correct because $\frac{7}{10}$ is more than $\frac{1}{2}$ and therefore rounds up to 1: 3,464 + 1 = 3,465, not 3,460.

6. The population of the city of Singapore is 2,812,000. What number is closest to the city's population?

● 2,800,000

This answer is correct because the difference between 2,800,000 and 2,812,000 is 12,000, which makes 2,800,000 the closest of all the answer choices.

Ⓑ 3,000,000

This answer is not correct because the difference between 3,000,000 and 2,812,000 is 188,000, which is more than 12,000.

Ⓒ 2,900,000

This answer is not correct because the difference between 2,900,000 and 2,812,000 is 88,000, which is more than 12,000.

Ⓓ 2,850,000

This answer is not correct because the difference between 2,850,000 and 2,812,000 is 38,000, which is more than 12,000.

You estimate amounts of money to find the nearest dollar.

▶ To estimate an amount of money to the nearest dollar, look at the exact amount and determine the number of cents. If the number of cents is 50 or greater, round the amount up to the next dollar. If the number of cents is less than 50, round the amount down, to the given dollar value.

Jack's class needed money for a field trip. They decided to raise money by washing cars. Do Numbers 7 through 10.

7. Jack made $8.31, including tips, at the car wash. About how many dollars did Jack contribute to the field-trip fund?
   Ⓐ $9.00
   Ⓑ $8.50
   Ⓒ $8.00
   Ⓓ $8.30

8. Jack's classmate Maria made $6.12 in the morning and $4.89 in the afternoon. To the nearest dollar, how much money did she make?
   Ⓐ $10.00
   Ⓑ $11.00
   Ⓒ $12.00
   Ⓓ $13.00

9. The total amount raised by Jack's class was $207.84. To the nearest dollar, how much money did they collect?
   Ⓐ $207
   Ⓑ $200
   Ⓒ $210
   Ⓓ $208

10. Jack's friend Sam rounded the amount he made to the nearest dollar. His estimate was $11. Which of the following could be his actual amount?
   Ⓐ $10.57
   Ⓑ $11.87
   Ⓒ $10.39
   Ⓓ $11.51

Jack compared prices at two different grocery stores in his town. Read this chart that Jack made about what he discovered. Then do Numbers 11 through 14.

ITEM	Market Up	Value Giant
loaf of bread	$1.69	$1.29
gallon of milk	$2.19	$1.89
one dozen eggs	$3.25	$1.99
head of lettuce	$0.79	$1.49

11. Jack noticed that if he estimated the price of a gallon of milk at each store, the prices were the same. Which estimate is the price of a gallon of milk at either store?

Ⓐ $1
Ⓑ $4
Ⓒ $2
Ⓓ $5

12. Jack estimated the total for the items at Market Up. To the nearest dollar, what was his correct estimate?

Ⓐ $ 7
Ⓑ $ 6
Ⓒ $10
Ⓓ $ 8

13. Jack estimated, to the nearest dollar, the total for the items at Value Giant. What was Jack's correct estimate?

Ⓐ $4
Ⓑ $6
Ⓒ $5
Ⓓ $7

14. Jack estimated, to the nearest dollar, the cost of 10 dozen eggs at Market Up. What was his correct estimate?

Ⓐ $30
Ⓑ $32
Ⓒ $28
Ⓓ $24

▶ A test question about estimation may ask you to round a number to its nearest ten, hundred, thousand, ten thousand, hundred thousand, or million, and so forth.

▶ A test question about estimation may ask you to tell the nearest whole number of a mixed number.

▶ A test question about estimation may require you to use rounding to estimate the answer to an addition or multiplication problem.

▶ A test question about estimation may ask you to estimate an amount of money to the nearest dollar.

Here are some facts that Jack learned about the Grand Canyon.
Read what Jack learned. Then do Numbers 15 and 16.

A Natural Wonder of the World

Grand Canyon National Park, in northwestern Arizona, covers 1,217,158 acres. The canyon is $199\frac{2}{5}$ miles long and an average of $10\frac{9}{10}$ miles wide. At its deepest point, it is $5,237\frac{4}{5}$ feet deep.

Using Estimation

15. Jack estimated, to the nearest ten thousand, the total number of acres of Grand Canyon National Park. What was his correct estimate?
   Ⓐ 1,210,000 acres
   Ⓑ 1,220,000 acres
   Ⓒ 1,217,000 acres
   Ⓓ 1,217,160 acres

Using Estimation

16. Jack used the canyon's length and width to estimate its area. He rounded the length to the nearest hundred and the width to the nearest whole number. What was his correct estimate of the area?
   Ⓐ 2,000 square miles
   Ⓑ 2,190 square miles
   Ⓒ 2,200 square miles
   Ⓓ 1,990 square miles

Jack read some statistics about baseball games. Read what Jack learned. Then do Numbers 17 and 18.

Take Me Out to the Ball Game

Going to baseball games has become very expensive. The national average price for a ticket is $21.37. A hot dog at a major-league ballpark costs an average of $2.74. A beverage costs another $4.12. The average price for a program is $11.85.

Even with the high cost, baseball is still America's favorite pastime. Yankee Stadium, with seating for 57,545, often sells every ticket.

Using Estimation

17. Jack also read that Yankee Stadium, in an average year, hosts 12 sold-out games. He wanted to know how many tickets, to the nearest thousand per game, would be sold for sold-out games in an average year. What was his correct estimate?

   Ⓐ 696,000 tickets
   Ⓑ 580,000 tickets
   Ⓒ 684,000 tickets
   Ⓓ 570,000 tickets

Using Estimation

18. Jack estimated, to the nearest dollar, how much money he would spend at an average game. He assumed that he would buy one hot dog, one beverage, and one program while he was at the game. What was his correct estimate?

   Ⓐ $38
   Ⓑ $41
   Ⓒ $40
   Ⓓ $42

PART ONE: Learn About Addition

Study the addition problem that Tony's teacher asked him to solve. As you study, think about the way that Tony followed to find the sum.

Problem: A dietitian weighed the ingredients in a sandwich. The ham weighed 1.712 oz; a piece of turkey weighed 2 oz; the cheese weighed 0.6667 oz; the lettuce weighed 0.008 oz; and the whole-grain bread weighed 2.4001 oz. How much did the entire sandwich weigh?

How Tony Solves the Problem	
I line up the decimal points of the addends.	$\begin{array}{r} \overset{1\ \ \ 1}{} \\ 1.7120 \\ 2.0000 \\ 0.6667 \\ 0.0080 \\ +2.4001 \\ \hline 6.7868 \end{array}$
I write the whole number, 2, with a decimal point and 4 zeroes. I put a zero to the right of the decimals to the ten thousands.	
I add from right to left. I regroup when a column adds up to more than 10.	
I include the decimal point in my answer unless the sum is a whole number.	

Answer: The entire sandwich weighed 6.7868 oz.

Addends may be added in any order without changing the sum.
Addends may be written in columns.

You use **addition** to find the sum of two or more addends.

▶ Put addends in any order and get the same sum.

▶ When writing addends, line up the place values. When addends are decimals, line up decimal points. When addends include both decimals and whole numbers, add a decimal point and zeroes to each whole number.

▶ When adding decimals that do not have matching place values, put one or more zeroes to the right of the decimal point so as to line up place values correctly.

▶ Add columns of addends from right to left. Regroup, if necessary. If the sum is a decimal, place the decimal point to the left of the tenths place.

**Study another one of Tony's problems. Look at how Tony solved the problem.
Then do Numbers 1 through 4.**

Problem: An accountant bought supplies for her home office. She bought a calculator for $127.00; a box of red pens for $12.05; a carton of paper for $23.88; a stapler for $6.49; and tape for $0.99. Put the items in columns. Then find what the accountant paid for all the supplies.

	Item	Price
Check that decimal points and place values line up in columns.	calculator	$127.00
Add from right to left	pens	$ 12.05
Regroup by 10s, if necessary.	paper	$ 23.88
Find the sum.	stapler	$ 6.49
	tape	$ 0.99
Write the decimal point in the sum.	Total	$170.41

Answer: The accountant paid $170.41 for all the supplies.

---

1. The chart shows what Tony spent for in-line skating equipment. How much did he spend all together?

Equipment	Cost
Skates	$106.38
Helmet	$ 64.50
Elbow Pads	$ 9.00
Knee Pads	$ 13.95

Ⓐ $ 173.21 Ⓒ $ 193.83
Ⓑ $1,084.13 Ⓓ $ 202.71

2. Tony enjoys skating in city parks. Ames Park has 13.012 miles of paths that in-line skaters can use. King Park has 8.148 miles of paths. Lincoln Park has 2.3601 miles of paths. How many miles of skating paths do the three parks have all together?

Ⓐ 12.047 miles   Ⓒ   2.4101 miles
Ⓑ 23.5201 miles Ⓓ 21.053 miles

3. Tony saw an ad in a magazine for a 4-week in-line skating program. How much would the program cost if Tony attended classes all 4 weeks?

Week 1	$56.00
Week 2	$49.00
Week 3	$35.00
Week 4	$30.00

Ⓐ $216   Ⓒ $170
Ⓑ $164   Ⓓ $155

4. In the first week of May, Tony skated for 256 minutes. In the second week, he skated for 493 minutes. In the third week, he skated for 531 minutes. How many minutes did he skate over the three weeks?

Ⓐ 1,280 minutes   Ⓒ 1,279 minutes
Ⓑ 1,180 minutes   Ⓓ 1,179 minutes

Work with a partner.

Talk about your answers to questions 1–4.
Tell why you chose the answers you did.

PART TWO: Check Your Understanding

Remember: You use addition to find the sum of two or more addends.

- ▶ Put addends in any order and get the same sum.
- ▶ When writing addends, line up the place values. When addends are decimals, line up decimal points. When addends include both decimals and whole numbers, add a decimal point and zeroes to each whole number.
- ▶ When adding decimals that do not have matching place values, put one or more zeroes to the right of the decimal point so as to line up place values correctly.
- ▶ Add columns of addends from right to left. Regroup, if necessary. If the sum is a decimal, place the decimal point to the left of the tenths place.

Solve this problem. As you work, ask yourself, "Have I lined up numbers by their place values? Should I add a zero at the end of a decimal to help me line up place values correctly?"

5. For each of three rainy days, Tony placed an empty cup outdoors. At the end of each day, he measured the rain in the cup. The first day, he measured 0.3175 cm; the second day, 0.094 cm; the third day, 0.008 cm. How much rain water did Tony measure in all?

Ⓐ 4.195 cm
Ⓑ 0.041 cm
Ⓒ 0.4195 cm
Ⓓ 0.3349 cm

Solve another problem. As you work, ask yourself, "Do I need to regroup? Is the sum a decimal or a whole number?"

6. Tony's father is a librarian. The chart shows the amount of fines he collected for overdue books during four months. What was the total amount of fines for all four months?

May	$52.85
June	$28.74
July	$44.99
August	$18.53

Ⓐ $152.11
Ⓑ $135.11
Ⓒ $144.91
Ⓓ $145.11

Look at the answer choices for each question.
Read why each answer choice is correct or not correct.

5. For each of three rainy days, Tony placed an empty cup outdoors. At the end of each day, he measured the rain in the cup. The first day, he measured 0.3175 cm; the second day, 0.094 cm; the third day, 0.008 cm. How much rain water did Tony measure in all?

Ⓐ 4.195 cm

   This answer is not correct because it is 3.7755 more than the actual sum. You may not have lined up the decimal points correctly.

Ⓑ 0.041 cm

   This answer is not correct because it is 0.3785 less than the actual sum. You may not have lined up the addends correctly.

● 0.4195 cm

   This answer is correct because the sum of 0.3175 + 0.094 + 0.008 = 0.4195. If you lined up the decimal points in the addends and added the columns correctly, you found the sum to be 0.4195.

Ⓓ 0.3349 cm

   This answer is not correct because it is 0.0846 less than the actual sum. You may have written 0.094 as .0094.

6. Tony's father is a librarian. The chart shows the amount of fines he collected for overdue books during four months. What was the total amount of fines for all four months?

May	$52.85
June	$28.74
July	$44.99
August	$18.53

Ⓐ $152.11

   This answer is not correct because it is $7.00 more than the actual sum. You may have added the ones column incorrectly.

Ⓑ $135.11

   This answer is not correct because it is $10.00 less than the actual sum. You may not have regrouped 10 ones as 1 ten.

Ⓒ $144.91

   This answer is not correct because it is $0.20 less than the actual sum. You may have added the tenths column incorrectly.

● $145.11

   This answer is correct because the sum of $52.85 + $28.74 + $44.99 + $18.53 = $145.11. If you added and regrouped each column correctly, you found the correct sum.

You use addition to find the sum of fractions.

▶ When you add fractions with common denominators, add the numerators. Write this sum over the common denominator.

▶ When you add fractions with different denominators, first change the fractions so that they have a common denominator. Then find the sum.

▶ When you add mixed numbers with different denominators, first find a common denominator for the fractions. Next, add the fractions. Then add the whole numbers.

▶ Always express the sum of fractions in lowest terms. To convert a fraction to a decimal, divide the numerator by the denominator and add a decimal point.

Add.	Find a common denominator.	Add fractions. Add whole numbers.	Express the sum in lowest terms.
$6\frac{1}{2}$ $7\frac{3}{4}$ $+\ 3\frac{4}{5}$	$6\frac{10}{20}$ $7\frac{15}{20}$ $+\ 3\frac{16}{20}$	$6\frac{10}{20}$ $7\frac{15}{20}$ $+\ 3\frac{16}{20}$ $16\frac{41}{20}$	$16\frac{41}{20} = 18\frac{1}{20},$ or 18.05

During a severe lightning storm, the power in Tony's house went out. While waiting for the power to be restored, Tony made up math problems. Do Numbers 7 through 10.

7. Tony timed three thunderclaps. The first rumbled for $8\frac{1}{3}$ seconds; the next one rumbled for $14\frac{1}{4}$ seconds; the last one rumbled for $22\frac{5}{8}$ seconds. How long did the three thunderclaps rumble all together?

   Ⓐ $44\frac{7}{24}$ seconds

   Ⓑ $45\frac{5}{24}$ seconds

   Ⓒ $44\frac{5}{8}$ seconds

   Ⓓ $45\frac{3}{8}$ seconds

8. Tony measured the length of 4 flashlights. From shortest to longest, the flashlights measured: $18\frac{2}{3}$ cm, $29\frac{1}{2}$ cm, $30\frac{1}{6}$ cm, and $35\frac{1}{5}$ cm. If Tony laid the flashlights end to end, what would their total length be?

   Ⓐ $113\frac{8}{15}$ cm

   Ⓑ $112\frac{1}{10}$ cm

   Ⓒ $112\frac{11}{30}$ cm

   Ⓓ $113\frac{1}{5}$ cm

9. During the storm, the power was out $75\frac{11}{12}$ minutes, and it stayed out $53\frac{3}{4}$ minutes more after the storm ended. The next morning, the power went out $109\frac{2}{3}$ minutes more. How long was the power out all together?

   Ⓐ $237\frac{2}{3}$ minutes   Ⓒ $239\frac{7}{12}$ minutes

   Ⓑ $238\frac{1}{4}$ minutes   Ⓓ $239\frac{1}{3}$ minutes

10. Tony read that 1 lightning strike equals about 250 kilowatt hours of electricity. The chart shows what 3 hours' worth of lightning strikes might be worth at the prices paid for electricity in his city. What amount is closest to the total of all 3 hours?

Hour	Amount
1	$301\frac{17}{18}$
2	$485\frac{1}{3}$
3	$519\frac{1}{6}$

   Ⓐ $1,396.34   Ⓒ $1,306.44

   Ⓑ $1,295.21   Ⓓ $1,316.01

After the storm, Tony borrowed books and articles about thunderstorms from the library. Read what Tony learned. Then do Numbers 11 through 14.

- Every day, about 45,000 thunderstorms occur worldwide. That's 16 million storms a year!

- An average thunderstorm travels at about 25 mph and is about 6 to 10 miles wide.

- An average storm "cell" lives for only 20 minutes. Long storms are the result of a series of cells.

- Severe storms are often accompanied by floods, high winds, and tornadoes.

11. Tony read about 3 tornadoes that touched down in a recent storm. The path of the first tornado was $62\frac{1}{2}$ yards wide; the second was $447\frac{5}{6}$ yards wide; the third was $704\frac{23}{36}$ yards wide. How wide would the 3 storms have been side by side?

Ⓐ $1,214\frac{35}{36}$ yards

Ⓑ $1,203\frac{29}{36}$ yards

Ⓒ $1,123\frac{5}{18}$ yards

Ⓓ $1,061\frac{1}{6}$ yards

12. Tony used this chart to figure out how long a thunderstorm, made up of 4 different cells, might last. To the nearest thousandth of a minute, how many minutes would the storm last?

Cell	Minutes
A	$19\frac{1}{4}$
B	$15\frac{3}{20}$
C	$11\frac{9}{10}$
D	$18\frac{5}{12}$

Ⓐ 63.826 minutes

Ⓑ 65.395 minutes

Ⓒ 63.430 minutes

Ⓓ 64.717 minutes

13. Tony tracked the speed of a tornado as reported on the weather channel. At 4:00 P.M., the tornado was traveling $38\frac{1}{2}$ mph; at 4:30 P.M., it was moving $6\frac{3}{4}$ mph faster; at 5:00 P.M., it was moving $12\frac{11}{16}$ mph faster than the last speed. What was the tornado's speed at 5:00 P.M.?

Ⓐ $56\frac{7}{8}$ mph

Ⓑ $57\frac{15}{16}$ mph

Ⓒ $56\frac{3}{4}$ mph

Ⓓ $57\frac{1}{2}$ mph

14. Tony learned that thunderstorms can also produce hail. The largest hailstone on record fell in Kansas and weighed $1\frac{2}{3}$ pounds. What is the total weight of hailstones A, B, and C?

Hailstone	Weight (in ounces)
A	$10\frac{13}{32}$
B	$12\frac{1}{4}$
C	$20\frac{5}{8}$

Ⓐ $43\frac{5}{16}$ oz

Ⓑ $42\frac{11}{32}$ oz

Ⓒ $43\frac{9}{32}$ oz

Ⓓ $42\frac{3}{8}$ oz

▶ A test question about addition may ask for the sum of decimals.

▶ A test question about addition may ask for the sum of numbers in columns.

▶ A test question about addition may ask for the sum of mixed numbers that have fractions with unlike denominators.

Every spring, students in Tony's school participate in Earth Day activities. Read some facts that Tony learned about our planet. Then do Numbers 15 and 16.

That's a Lot of Rubbish

People in the United States make more trash than people anywhere else in the world. Each person in America throws out about 1,600 pounds of trash per year! However, young people all over the world are organizing and participating in recycling projects and other programs to help protect and preserve our environment.

Applying Addition

15. Tony used the following figures to find how many pounds of trash per person that people in 5 countries produce daily: U.S., 4.343 lb; Australia, 4.1667 lb; Canada, 3.81 lb; Switzerland, 3.616 lb; France, 3.6 lb. What amount is the correct sum per person for the 5 countries?

   Ⓐ 18.4252 lb per person
   Ⓑ 18.0111 lb per person
   Ⓒ 19.5357 lb per person
   Ⓓ 19.0978 lb per person

Applying Addition

16. Tony's class organized a fund-raiser to support programs that protect endangered animals. The chart shows how much money the class collected in 4 days. How much money was collected in all?

Day	Amount
Wed.	$308.97
Thurs.	$181.06
Fri.	$273.50
Sat.	$415.00

   Ⓐ $1,178.53
   Ⓑ $1,097.41
   Ⓒ $1,062.43
   Ⓓ $1,182.51

Tony's teacher asked students to write a biography of a famous conservationist. Read part of what Tony wrote. Then do Numbers 17 and 18.

Theodore Roosevelt: A President for the Environment

Theodore Roosevelt was born in 1858 in New York City. Even as a young boy, Roosevelt was fascinated by nature. At age 9, because he had what he thought was an impressive collection of seashells, birds' nests, dead insects, and rocks, he started his own museum in his parents' apartment. He called it the Roosevelt Museum of Natural History. Roosevelt remained interested in nature and when he became president, in 1901, he used the power of his office to protect and preserve the natural beauty of America. During his presidency, he created 5 national parks, 18 national monuments, and 51 wildlife refuges. Because of all his work to protect our environment, Roosevelt is sometimes called the Conservation President.

Applying Addition

17. Tony made this chart to show the approximate size of three of the national parks Roosevelt created. How many acres do the three parks cover in all?

Park	Acres (in thousands)
Crater Lake	$28\frac{3}{10}$
Wind Cave	$52\frac{1}{8}$
Mesa Verde	$183\frac{1}{5}$

Ⓐ $254\frac{13}{20}$ thousand acres

Ⓑ $153\frac{3}{4}$ thousand acres

Ⓒ $263\frac{5}{8}$ thousand acres

Ⓓ $264\frac{7}{10}$ thousand acres

Applying Addition

18. Tony made two trips to the library. On his first visit, he spent $2\frac{1}{2}$ hours finding books and $1\frac{1}{4}$ hours taking notes. The next visit, he spent 2 hours finding articles and $3\frac{5}{6}$ hours taking notes. He also spent $4\frac{2}{3}$ hours on the Internet. What was the total time Tony spent doing research and taking notes?

Ⓐ $12\frac{11}{12}$ hours

Ⓑ $14\frac{1}{4}$ hours

Ⓒ $13\frac{1}{6}$ hours

Ⓓ $13\frac{1}{2}$ hours

PART ONE: Read a Story

Here is a story about Rudy's social-studies project. Read the story.
Then do Numbers 1 through 6.

A School Project

"Your assignment," Rudy's social-studies teacher said, "is to prepare a report about an important community issue. Choose a topic that interests you, something that you'd like to learn more about. For example, you might write about the new youth center."

Rudy's friend Gina decided to write about the youth center. Rudy, however, figured that he already knew as much as he wanted to know about the subject. His mother, who was an architect, was on the center's design committee.

But by the time Rudy got home from school that afternoon, he still hadn't come up with a good topic for his report. Then he saw a sign that his dad had taped over the kitchen sink. The sign said REMEMBER THE WATER SHORTAGE! DO NOT LEAVE THE WATER RUNNING WHEN WASHING DISHES OR GETTING A DRINK. Rudy found another sign in the bathroom. CONSERVE WATER. DO NOT TAKE LONG SHOWERS. THAT MEANS YOU, RUDY.

Rudy laughed. Then he recalled a conversation he had overheard on the bus the day before. Two men were discussing the water ban. "My lawn is so dry and yellow that it looks like a giant straw mat," one man said.

"The dust on my car is an inch thick," the other man complained. "The reservoir is way below normal levels. If it doesn't rain soon, we may have to cut out daily showers. Of course, my youngest son won't mind in the least," the man joked.

Rudy had never thought about the connection between rain and the water he drank and used to shower. He also had never questioned how the water ended up at his house. Suddenly, Rudy realized he had found his report topic.

The next day, Rudy visited the local water-works department. The department manager explained to Rudy that water flows from far-off mountains, through rivers and streams, and into man-made reservoirs, or giant lakes. From there, it travels through huge pipes called aqueducts to the city's main water pipes and, finally, to the water pipes that lead to homes, businesses, and schools.

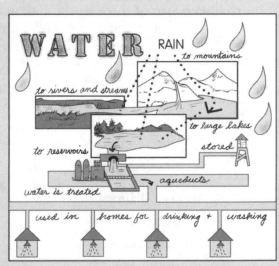

Rudy enjoyed gathering facts for his project. He created a map to illustrate the journey that water traveled to reach people's homes. He interviewed classmates, family members, and other people in the community to find out what they knew about water and what they were doing to conserve it.

He also began taking shorter showers.

Building Number Sense

1. Rudy found out that the city gets its water from three different reservoirs. The Sugar Hill Reservoir provides about $\frac{2}{7}$ of the city's daily water needs. The Cretan Dam Reservoir provides about $\frac{11}{42}$ of the city's needs. What fraction shows the sum of $\frac{2}{7}$ and $\frac{11}{42}$?

Ⓐ $\frac{13}{14}$ Ⓒ $\frac{3}{7}$

Ⓑ $\frac{22}{49}$ Ⓓ $\frac{23}{42}$

Building Number Sense

2. Rudy learned that the three reservoirs also provide water to the 965,423 people who live in the counties surrounding the city. Which of these represents the value of the 96 in 965,423?

Ⓐ 9.6×10^7

Ⓑ 9.6×10^9

Ⓒ 9.6×10^5

Ⓓ 9.6×10^6

Using Estimation

3. Rudy and Gina went shopping for supplies for a report they were doing. As they shopped, they rounded the cost of each item listed below to the nearest dollar. What was their correct estimate for all the items?

  2 audiocassettes—$1.58 each
  2 large poster boards—$0.85 each
  1 pkg. markers—$3.97 each

Ⓐ $12   Ⓒ $5

Ⓑ $10   Ⓓ $9

Using Estimation

4. Rudy figured out that if each of the 524 apartments in a city complex had a leaky faucet, about 20,436 gallons of water would be wasted in 1 week. He rounded this number to the nearest hundred. How much water would be wasted in 1 year?

Ⓐ 1,060,800 gal   Ⓒ 1,063,000 gal

Ⓑ 1,070,000 gal   Ⓓ 1,062,500 gal

Applying Addition

5. Through conservation, four of Rudy's neighbors saved money on their annual water bill. How much did the neighbors save all together?

Neighbor	Savings
A	$ 97.36
B	$194.00
C	$301.09
D	$265.50

Ⓐ $864.41   Ⓒ $748.85

Ⓑ $857.95   Ⓓ $760.91

Applying Addition

6. Rudy included the following chart on his poster. How many square miles in all do the three reservoirs cover?

Reservoir	Square Miles
Sugar Hill	$572\frac{1}{2}$
Cretan Dam	$524\frac{7}{12}$
Laurel	$900\frac{2}{3}$

Ⓐ $1,994\frac{5}{6}$ sq mi   Ⓒ $1,996\frac{5}{6}$ sq mi

Ⓑ $1,995\frac{11}{12}$ sq mi   Ⓓ $1,997\frac{3}{4}$ sq mi

Here is part of an article that Freida read about oceans.
Read the article. Then do Numbers 7 through 12.

Water, water everywhere/Nor any drop to drink.
—from *The Rime of the Ancient Mariner*, by Samuel Taylor Coleridge

If you were fortunate enough to travel into space some day, you would have the great privilege of looking down on Earth. Then you could verify that, indeed, water is just about everywhere on the planet. More than 70% of Earth's surface is covered by water. Most of that water is salt water that is contained in the earth's four oceans: the Pacific, the Atlantic, the Indian, and the Arctic.

The Pacific Ocean is the world's largest ocean. Located between Antarctica, Asia, Australia, and the Western Hemisphere, the Pacific Ocean covers an area of about 165,250,000 sq km and has an average depth of 4,280 m. The Mariana Trench, which is in the Pacific Ocean, is 11,034 m deep; it is the deepest known place in the world. To understand how large the Pacific Ocean is, think about this: If you put all the land in the world together, the total area of the land would not be as large as the Pacific Ocean.

The Atlantic Ocean, the world's second largest ocean, forms the eastern coastlines of North and South America and the western coastlines of Europe and Africa. Along with its many seas—which include the Caribbean Sea, the Gulf of Mexico, the Mediterranean Sea, and the Black Sea—the Atlantic Ocean covers about 20% of Earth's surface, or an area of 106,460,000 sq km. Its average depth is 3,300 m. You might be surprised to learn that the Atlantic Ocean is home to one of the world's great mountain ranges. The Mid-Atlantic Ridge stretches the entire length of the Atlantic. Although most of the Mid-Atlantic Ridge is under 2,700 m of water, some of it extends above the water's surface to form islands, such as Iceland and the Azores.

The Indian Ocean is the third largest ocean in the world. It covers an area of 73,440,000 sq km and has an average depth of 3,890 m. The Indian Ocean extends between the southernmost parts of Africa and Australia.

The Arctic Ocean, which covers an area of 12,257,000 sq km, is the world's smallest ocean. Parts of the Arctic Ocean, which is located on the North Pole, are permanently frozen. The ice is made up of glacier ice and sea ice that, by the end of the Arctic winter, may be as much as 10 ft thick. When sea ice forms, it gradually loses salt. Eventually, it has so little salt that it can be melted and used for drinking.

Building Number Sense

7. Freida read that about $\frac{11}{20}$ of the world's fish supply comes from the Pacific Ocean. She also discovered that people get approximately $\frac{1}{6}$ of their animal protein from fish. What is $\frac{1}{6} \times \frac{11}{20}$?

ⓐ $\frac{1}{36}$

ⓑ $\frac{11}{120}$

ⓒ $\frac{6}{13}$

ⓓ $\frac{13}{120}$

Building Number Sense

8. One article that Freida read said that the Arctic Ocean is about 1.5 times the size of the U.S. Another article said that it is 1.286 times the size of the U.S. What is the place value of the 8 in 1.286?

ⓐ 8 tenths

ⓑ 8 hundredths

ⓒ 8

ⓓ 80

Using Estimation

9. Freida rounded the size of the Arctic Ocean to the nearest hundred thousand square kilometers. What was her correct estimate?

ⓐ 12,200,000 sq km

ⓑ 12,350,000 sq km

ⓒ 12,260,000 sq km

ⓓ 12,300,000 sq km

Using Estimation

10. While studying a map of Iceland, Freida figured out that the island's average distance from east to west is $268\frac{1}{3}$ miles, and from north to south is $147\frac{5}{6}$ miles. Freida used these figures to estimate Iceland's area. She rounded the distance from east to west to the nearest ten, and from north to south to the nearest whole number. What was her correct estimate?

ⓐ 39,500 sq mi   ⓒ 39,960 sq mi

ⓑ 39,650 sq mi   ⓓ 39,000 sq mi

Applying Addition

11. Freida learned that until 1899, the deepest known part of the Mariana Trench was 9.66 km. In 1929, an area 0.153 km deeper was found. Then, in the late 1950's, the deepest part was found; it was 1.221 km deeper than the spot found in 1929. How deep is the deepest known spot?

ⓐ 12.411 km

ⓑ   9.95 km

ⓒ 10.43 km

ⓓ 11.034 km

Applying Addition

12. Freida made this chart to show the approximate size of the three largest seas. How many sq km do the three seas cover in all?

Sea	Sq Km (in millions)
Mediterranean	$2\frac{9}{10}$
Caribbean	$2\frac{3}{4}$
South China Sea	$2\frac{1}{3}$

ⓐ $7\frac{59}{60}$ million sq km

ⓑ $8\frac{13}{30}$ million sq km

ⓒ $7\frac{1}{2}$ million sq km

ⓓ $6\frac{4}{5}$ million sq km

APPLYING SUBTRACTION

PART ONE: Learn About Subtraction

**Study the problem that Val's teacher wrote on the board.
As you study, think about the way that Val solved it.**

Problem: Mrs. Franco stopped to pick up two pizzas on her way home from work. She gave the cashier a 50-dollar bill and a coupon for $1.98 off the price of two pizzas. The cost of the two pizzas with the coupon was $14.52. How much change did Mrs. Franco get?

How Val Solves the Problem	
I read the problem carefully to be sure I know what number to subtract.	$50.00 − 14.52 $35.48
I line up the decimal points and write the whole dollar amount with a decimal point and two zeroes.	
I subtract the columns from right to left. I regroup when the number I am subtracting is larger than the number I am subtracting from.	
I write the dollar sign and decimal point in the answer.	

Answer: Mrs. Franco got $35.48 in change.

When you subtract, you find the difference between two numbers. The difference is always smaller than the number subtracted from, unless you subtract 0.

You use subtraction to find out how many are left or how many more are needed. You also use subtraction to make comparisons. For example, you can use subtraction to compare distances, heights, weights, and other amounts.

You use **subtraction** to find the difference between two numbers.

▶ When writing numbers in a subtraction problem, line up the numbers according to their place values.

▶ When subtracting decimals or money, line up the decimal points. If one of the numbers is a whole number and the other number is a decimal, write the whole number with a decimal point and one or more zeroes.

▶ Subtract from right to left. Regroup, if necessary. If the difference is a decimal, write the decimal point to the left of the tenths place.

Study another one of Val's problems. Look at how Val solved the problem. Then do Numbers 1 through 4.

Problem: Before Aaron removed 4 CDs, with a combined playing time of 151.33 minutes, from a CD player, there were 12 CDs in the player. The total playing time for all 12 CDs was 460.4 minutes. What is the playing time for the remaining 8 CDs?

Write the problem so that the smaller number is to be subtracted from the larger number. Line up decimal points and place values, and add a zero in the hundredths column.

$$\begin{array}{r} \scriptstyle 5\ 10\ 3\ 10 \\ 4\cancel{6}\cancel{0}.\cancel{4}\cancel{0} \\ -\ 151.33 \\ \hline 309.07 \end{array}$$

Subtract from right to left, starting with the hundredths column. Regroup, if necessary.

Write the decimal point in the difference.

Answer: The playing time for the 8 CDs is 309.07 minutes.

1. Val's house is 320.43 ft from town hall. Her grandparents' house is 518 ft from town hall. How much closer is Val's house to the town hall?
   - Ⓐ 208.67 ft
   - Ⓑ 197.57 ft
   - Ⓒ 218.63 ft
   - Ⓓ 198.67 ft

2. When Val's grandparents moved to town in 1968, they paid $52,785 for a house. Ten years later, they sold that house for $99,600. How much profit did they earn on the sale of the house?
   - Ⓐ $51,185
   - Ⓑ $36,905
   - Ⓒ $47,385
   - Ⓓ $46,815

3. The Hill Valley Mall in Val's town originally took up 90 acres. Last year, the mall was enlarged by 50%. It now covers 135 acres. How much land was needed to enlarge the mall?
   - Ⓐ 45 acres
   - Ⓑ 40 acres
   - Ⓒ 85 acres
   - Ⓓ 50 acres

4. Val's parents now pay $24.57 in real-estate taxes for each thousand dollars that their house is worth. Over the last four years, the tax rate rose by $5.00. What was the tax rate four years ago, before the rate hikes?
   - Ⓐ $29.57 per thousand
   - Ⓑ $20.57 per thousand
   - Ⓒ $19.57 per thousand
   - Ⓓ $ 9.57 per thousand

Work with a partner.

Talk about your answers to questions 1–4. Tell why you chose the answers you did.

Remember: You use subtraction to find the difference between two numbers.

▶ When writing numbers in a subtraction problem, line up the numbers according to their place values.

▶ When subtracting decimals or money, line up the decimal points. If one of the numbers is a whole number and the other number is a decimal, write the whole number with a decimal point and one or more zeroes.

▶ Subtract from right to left. Regroup, if necessary. If the difference is a decimal, write the decimal point to the left of the tenths place.

Solve this problem. As you work, ask yourself, "What number do I subtract? Have I lined up the numbers by their place values? Did I subtract each column correctly?"

5. Val's grandfather paid $35 for a painting at a flea market. An art dealer offered $3,750 for the painting. An expert said the actual value of the painting was 12 thousand dollars. What is the difference between the art dealer's offer and the painting's actual value?

   Ⓐ $ 8,250
   Ⓑ $11,625
   Ⓒ $ 23.00
   Ⓓ $ 9,350

Solve another problem. As you work, ask yourself, "Have I lined up the numbers by their place values and decimal points? Do I need to regroup? Is the difference a decimal or a whole number?"

6. At an antiques fair, Val's grandfather bought a 1950s toy fire truck, in excellent condition, for $69.94. A month earlier, a woman paid $91.76 for a similar truck in poorer condition. How much less did Val's grandfather pay?

   Ⓐ $32.62
   Ⓑ $22.82
   Ⓒ $21.82
   Ⓓ $21

Look at the answer choices for each question.
Read why each answer choice is correct or not correct.

5. Val's grandfather paid $35 for a painting at a flea market. An art dealer offered $3,750 for the painting. An expert said the actual value of the painting was 12 thousand dollars. What is the difference between the art dealer's offer and the painting's actual value?

● $8,250

This answer is correct because $12,000 - $3,750 = $8,250. If you lined up the numbers correctly and subtracted each column correctly, you found the difference to be $8,250.

Ⓑ $11,625

This answer is not correct because it is $3,375 more than the actual difference. You may not have lined up the numbers correctly, and may have subtracted $375 instead of $3,750.

Ⓒ $23.00

This answer is not correct because it is $8,227 less than the actual difference. You may have subtracted 12 from 35.

Ⓓ $9,350

This answer is not correct because it is $1,100 more than the actual difference. You may not have subtracted the hundreds or thousands columns correctly.

6. At an antiques fair, Val's grandfather bought a 1950s toy fire truck, in excellent condition, for $69.94. A month earlier, a woman paid $91.76 for a similar truck in poorer condition. How much less did Val's grandfather pay?

Ⓐ $32.62

This answer is not correct because it is $10.80 more than the actual difference. You may not have subtracted or regrouped correctly.

Ⓑ $22.82

This answer is not correct because it is $1 more than the actual difference. You may not have regrouped correctly.

● $21.82

This answer is correct because $91.76 - $69.94 = $21.82. If you subtracted and regrouped correctly, you found the correct difference.

Ⓓ $21

This answer is not correct because it is $0.82 less than the actual difference. The correct answer is not a whole-dollar amount; the decimal and cents are needed.

You use subtraction to find the difference between mixed numbers.

▶ To subtract a mixed number from a whole number, convert the whole number to a mixed number. Subtract the fractions, and then subtract the whole numbers.

▶ To subtract a mixed number from a mixed number, first find a common denominator for the fractions. If the fraction you are subtracting is greater than the fraction you are subtracting from, regroup one 1 to an improper fraction. Subtract the fractions, and then subtract the whole numbers.

▶ Express the difference of fractions in lowest terms.

Subtract.	Find a common denominator for fractions.	Regroup one 1 to an improper fraction.	Subtract the fractions. Subtract the whole numbers.
$12\frac{3}{9}$ $-7\frac{17}{18}$	$12\frac{6}{18}$ $-7\frac{17}{18}$	$11\frac{24}{18}$ $-7\frac{17}{18}$	$11\frac{24}{18}$ $-7\frac{17}{18}$ $\overline{4\frac{7}{18}}$

Val's art class painted wall murals in the school cafeteria. Do Numbers 7 through 10.

7. The mural that Val helped paint on one cafeteria wall is $27\frac{9}{10}$ meters from end to end. The wall is $31\frac{2}{5}$ meters long. How much of the available wall space was *not* used for the mural?
   Ⓐ $4\frac{11}{15}$ meters
   Ⓑ $3\frac{1}{2}$ meters
   Ⓒ $3\frac{7}{10}$ meters
   Ⓓ $4\frac{3}{5}$ meters

8. Val made a paper frame with a perimeter of 128 inches for one of the mural "photos" painted to look like a series of school photographs. To make the frame, Val cut 4 strips from a length of paper $144\frac{5}{6}$ inches long. How long was the remaining piece of paper?
   Ⓐ $16\frac{5}{6}$ inches
   Ⓑ $15\frac{1}{6}$ inches
   Ⓒ $14\frac{2}{3}$ inches
   Ⓓ $26\frac{5}{6}$ inches

9. Val, who is $155\frac{1}{2}$ cm tall, had to use a ladder to finish painting a tree that starts at the very bottom of the wall and stretches $213\frac{1}{3}$ cm up. What is the difference between Val's height and the height of the tree?
   Ⓐ $42\frac{2}{5}$ cm
   Ⓑ $58\frac{1}{6}$ cm
   Ⓒ $168\frac{2}{3}$ cm
   Ⓓ $57\frac{5}{6}$ cm

10. Val's art teacher gave students 32 cans of paint, including 9 cans of white paint and 6 cans of blue paint. After the mural was complete, $3\frac{1}{4}$ cans of white paint and $1\frac{2}{3}$ cans of blue paint were left over. How many cans of white paint were used for the mural?
    Ⓐ $8\frac{1}{3}$ cans
    Ⓑ $5\frac{1}{3}$ cans
    Ⓒ $5\frac{3}{4}$ cans
    Ⓓ $2\frac{3}{4}$ cans

Read what Val discovered about publishing a school newspaper. Then do Numbers 11 through 14.

Val enjoys writing and taking pictures, so she volunteered to work on the school newspaper. She thought she might like to be a reporter. Val's teacher, Ms. Lynnsi, suggested that since Val also has excellent math skills, she would make a good managing editor. At first, Val didn't understand how math skills would help her publish a newspaper. She soon learned.

11. Val studied previous editions of the 8-page school paper. She saw that in each issue, $1\frac{7}{8}$ of the pages were used for photos and cartoons, and $3\frac{1}{2}$ of the pages were used for school ads. How much more space was devoted to ads than to photos and cartoons?

  Ⓐ $1\frac{1}{2}$ pages

  Ⓑ $2\frac{2}{3}$ pages

  Ⓒ $1\frac{5}{8}$ pages

  Ⓓ $2\frac{3}{4}$ pages

12. As she continued to study the paper, Val figured that $5\frac{3}{8}$ of the paper's 8 pages were being used for ads, photos, and cartoons. How many pages did she figure were left for stories and articles?

  Ⓐ $2\frac{5}{8}$ pages

  Ⓑ $3\frac{3}{8}$ pages

  Ⓒ $3\frac{5}{8}$ pages

  Ⓓ $2\frac{3}{8}$ pages

13. With her teacher's guidance, Val redesigned the paper, providing more space for stories and articles. Her first issue as managing editor contained $306\frac{1}{5}$ lines of text. The previous issue had just $94\frac{1}{2}$ lines. How many more lines of text were in Val's first issue than were in the previous issue?

  Ⓐ $192\frac{2}{3}$ lines

  Ⓑ $212\frac{1}{2}$ lines

  Ⓒ $201\frac{2}{5}$ lines

  Ⓓ $211\frac{7}{10}$ lines

14. In previous issues, the cartoon on page 1 of the paper was $17\frac{1}{4}$ cm wide and $10\frac{3}{4}$ cm deep. Val decided to crop $7\frac{1}{4}$ cm from the width and $3\frac{9}{10}$ cm from the depth. What were the new dimensions of the cartoon?

  Ⓐ $14\frac{4}{5}$ cm wide $\times$ $3\frac{1}{2}$ cm deep

  Ⓑ $10\frac{1}{4}$ cm wide $\times$ $6\frac{1}{5}$ cm deep

  Ⓒ 10 cm wide $\times$ $6\frac{17}{20}$ cm deep

  Ⓓ $4\frac{1}{10}$ cm wide $\times$ $7\frac{1}{2}$ cm deep

▶ A test question about subtraction may ask you to subtract decimals or money.

▶ A test question about subtraction may ask you to subtract mixed and whole numbers.

Read about the special invitation that Val's school band received. Then do Numbers 15 and 16.

Strike Up the Band

Each year, five middle-school bands from around the state are chosen to march in a huge Thanksgiving Day parade in the state capital. Only the top marching bands are invited. Because of its history and size, the parade is televised all around the country. This year, Val's school band received an invitation. Band members, school officials, and town residents were honored that the band was selected.

Applying Subtraction

15. The exact cost for the 45 band members, 3 band teachers, and 6 adult chaperones to attend the parade was $23,456.41. Through a book sale, a raffle, and other events, students raised $11,786.84. State organizations offered to fund the rest. How much of this funding did Val's band need?

    Ⓐ $12,770.43
    Ⓑ $11,669.57
    Ⓒ $11,330.27
    Ⓓ $11,760.56

Applying Subtraction

16. The distance from Val's town to the state capital is 366.53 miles. After 2 hours on the road, the bus carrying the band had traveled 124.08 miles. An hour later, Val saw a sign that said the state capital was 190 miles away. How far had the bus gone in that last hour?

    Ⓐ 176.53 miles
    Ⓑ 31.40 miles
    Ⓒ 242.45 miles
    Ⓓ 52.45 miles

Val sent a postcard home to her parents after the parade.
Read Val's postcard message. Then do Numbers 17 and 18.

Dear Mom and Dad,

   How was Thanksgiving dinner without me? I bet there was a lot more food left over than usual. At the end of the parade, we were served a wonderful dinner with turkey, stuffing, cranberry sauce, sweet potatoes, corn, and salad. We ate in a huge tent set up in the city park. The food was pretty good, but I was almost too exhausted to eat. Dana, Annie, and I had stayed up very late talking the night before. We got up the next morning at 4:30 to get to the parade grounds. Then we had to march for $5\frac{1}{3}$ miles! Did you see me on TV? We were in the first $\frac{1}{4}$ mile of the parade, right behind the car carrying the governor and her husband. Every time I saw that the TV cameras were on us, I was playing my trombone, so I couldn't wave. I'll probably be home before this postcard arrives. So long.

                          Love,

                          Val

Applying Subtraction

17. Although Val's band marched $5\frac{1}{3}$ miles in $4\frac{1}{6}$ hours, students were not playing their instruments the whole time. Val figured that they played for about $2\frac{3}{4}$ hours. About how much time were they marching without playing?

    Ⓐ $1\frac{5}{12}$ hours

    Ⓑ $2\frac{7}{12}$ hours

    Ⓒ $1\frac{1}{6}$ hours

    Ⓓ $3\frac{1}{3}$ hours

Applying Subtraction

18. Mr. Amos, one of the chaperones, videotaped parts of the parade and other events of the trip. He edited out $129\frac{3}{4}$ minutes of the video and gave copies to band members. The unedited video was $184\frac{3}{20}$ minutes long. How long was the edited version?

    Ⓐ $65\frac{3}{10}$ minutes

    Ⓑ 64 minutes

    Ⓒ $54\frac{2}{5}$ minutes

    Ⓓ $55\frac{1}{5}$ minutes

Strategy Five APPLYING MULTIPLICATION

PART ONE: Learn About Multiplication

Study the problem that Luis's teacher wrote on the board. As you study, think about the way that Luis solved it.

Problem: 46.27 × 13

How Luis Solves the Problem

I write the factors in columns. I ignore the decimal point for now.

I multiply the top factor by the ones digit of the bottom factor. I write the partial product.

I put a zero as a placeholder in the ones column, and multiply the top factor by the tens digit of the bottom factor. I write the partial product.

I add the partial products and write the decimal point so that the number of decimal places in the product is the same as the total number of decimal places in the factors.

$$
\begin{array}{r}
46\underline{.27} \text{— decimal places =} \\
\times\ 13 \\
\hline
138\ 81 \\
+\ 462\ 70 \\
\hline
601.51 \text{— product}
\end{array}
$$

partial products

Answer: 46.27 × 13 = 601.51

Use the same strategy as above if one factor is an amount of money. Convert cents to hundredths.

Write the factors so that their right-most digit lines up. Then multiply by the digits in the bottom factor, from right to left. Ignore the decimal points while you multiply.

When multiplying by the tens digit, write a zero as a placeholder in the ones place of the partial product. Add the partial products.

Write the decimal point so that the number of decimal places in the product is the same as the total number of decimal places in the factors.

You use **multiplication** to find the product of two factors. A factor may be a decimal.

▶ Write the factors in columns, ignore any decimal points, solve for and add the partial products, and then place the decimal point.

▶ The number of decimal places in the product is the same as the total number of decimal places in the factors.

Study another one of Luis's problems. Think about the way that Luis solved the problem. Then do Numbers 1 through 4.

Problem: $17.85 × 23

> I write the factors in columns. I ignore the decimal point for now.
>
> I find and then add the partial products. I use a zero as a placeholder when multiplying by the tens digit.
>
> I write the decimal point so that the number of decimal places in the product is the same as the total number of decimal places in the factors.

$$
\begin{array}{r}
\$17.85 \\
\times\ 23 \\
\hline
53\ 55 \\
+\ 357\ 00 \\
\hline
\$410.55
\end{array}
$$

Answer: $17.85 × 23 = $410.55

1. Luis's parents own a garden store. His mother arranged 12 potted plants, at the price of $7.95 each, including tax, on a shelf. How much would all 12 plants cost?
   - Ⓐ $ 9.54
   - Ⓑ $ 95.40
   - Ⓒ $238.50
   - Ⓓ $ 23.85

2. Luis put price tags on vegetable seedlings. He counted 54 trays of green pepper seedlings. Each tray had a price of 99¢, including tax. What would be the total price for all of the trays?
   - Ⓐ $53.46
   - Ⓑ $ 9.72
   - Ⓒ $97.20
   - Ⓓ $ 5.35

3. Luis's father arranged 21 small bags of soil in a pile. Each bag contained 3.65 pounds of soil. What was the weight of the entire pile of soil?
   - Ⓐ 109.50 lb
   - Ⓑ 765.50 lb
   - Ⓒ 10.95 lb
   - Ⓓ 76.65 lb

4. One customer bought 44 tulip bulbs. Each bulb cost $1.33, including tax. What was the total cost of the bulbs?
   - Ⓐ $ 5.85
   - Ⓑ $ 10.64
   - Ⓒ $ 58.52
   - Ⓓ $106.40

 **Work with a partner.**

Talk about your answers to questions 1–4. Tell why you chose the answers you did.

Remember: You use multiplication to find the product of two factors. A factor may be a decimal.

▶ Write the factors in columns, ignore any decimal points, solve for and add the partial products, and then place the decimal point.

▶ The number of decimal places in the product is the same as the total number of decimal places in the factors.

Solve this problem. As you work, ask yourself, "How do I write and add the partial products?"

5. Luis's mother ordered 86 rakes from a wholesale garden-supply company. The price of each rake was $12.47. What was the total cost of the rakes, without tax?

   Ⓐ $ 174.58

   Ⓑ $1,072.42

   Ⓒ $ 925.02

   Ⓓ $ 961.42

Solve another problem. As you work, ask yourself, "Where do I write the decimal point in the product?"

6. Luis put price tags on 45 of the rakes. The store's price was $14.50 per rake. What would be the total price for all 45 rakes, without tax?

   Ⓐ $ 6.53

   Ⓑ $6,525.00

   Ⓒ $ 65.25

   Ⓓ $ 652.50

Look at the answer choices for each question.
Read why each answer choice is correct or not correct.

5. Luis's mother ordered 86 rakes from a wholesale garden-supply company. The price of each rake was $12.47. What was the total cost of the rakes, without tax?

Ⓐ $174.58

This answer is not correct because the partial products of 12.47 × 86 are 7482 + 99760. After the decimal point is placed, their sum is 1,072.42, not 174.58. You may have forgotten the placeholder in the partial product.

● $1,072.42

This answer is correct because it is the sum of the partial products 7482 + 99760.

Ⓒ $925.02

This answer is not correct because the partial products of 12.47 × 86 are 7482 + 99760. After the decimal point is placed, their sum is 1,072.42, not 925.02. You may have solved incorrectly for one or both of the partial products.

Ⓓ $961.42

This answer is not correct because the partial products of 12.47 × 86 are 7482 + 99760. After the decimal point is placed, their sum is 1,072.42, not 961.42. You may have solved incorrectly for one or both of the partial products.

6. Luis put price tags on 45 of the rakes. The store's price was $14.50 per rake. What would be the total price for all 45 rakes, without tax?

Ⓐ $6.53

This answer is not correct because $14.50 × 45 = $652.50. Because there are 2 decimal places in the factors, there are 2 decimal places in the product. Maybe you put 4 decimal places in the product and then rounded.

Ⓑ $6,525.00

This answer is not correct because $14.50 × 45 = $652.50. Because there are 2 decimal places in the factors, there are 2 decimal places in the product. Maybe you put 1 decimal place in the product and added a zero.

Ⓒ $65.25

This answer is not correct because $14.50 × 45 = $652.50. Because there are 2 decimal places in the factors, there are 2 decimal places in the product. Maybe you put 3 decimal places in the product and dropped the zero.

● $652.50

This answer is correct because $14.50 × 45 = $652.50. There are 2 decimal places in the factors, so there are 2 decimal places in the product.

In some multiplication problems, a factor can be a fraction, a mixed number, or a percent.

▶ Convert fractions, mixed numbers, or percents to decimals. Then write the factors in columns and solve as usual.

Fractions or Mixed Numbers → Decimals		Percents → Decimals
$\frac{1}{5}$ = 0.2	$\frac{1}{4}$ = 0.25	*percent* equals *hundredths*
$\frac{2}{5}$ = 0.4	$2\frac{1}{2}$ = 2.5	8% equals 8 hundredths = 0.08
$\frac{3}{5}$ = 0.6	$\frac{3}{4}$ = 0.75	25% equals 25 hundredths = 0.25
$\frac{4}{5}$ = 0.8	$1\frac{1}{4}$ = 1.25	74% equals 74 hundredths = 0.74

▶ One strategy to find the total cost of an item, including sales tax, is to multiply the price by (1 + sales tax %). For example, to find the total cost of an item with a sales tax of 5%, multiply the price by (1 + 0.05), or 1.05. So, the total cost of an item with a price of $5.00 and a 5% sales tax would be $5.00 × 1.05. This is the same as $5.00 + ($5.00 × 0.05). Both ways of solving produce the same answer: $5.25. When solving problems involving amounts of money, round your answer to hundredths (cents).

Luis conducted a survey about the hobbies of the students in his school.
Do Numbers 7 through 10.

7. Luis found that 85% of the students play at least one sport. There are 540 students. How many students play a sport?
   Ⓐ 216 students
   Ⓑ 486 students
   Ⓒ 459 students
   Ⓓ 46 students

8. The favorite hobby of some students is playing video games. One game sells for $39.99, plus 5% sales tax. What is the total cost of the video game?
   Ⓐ $59.99
   Ⓑ $41.99
   Ⓒ $40.04
   Ⓓ $49.54

9. Luis learned that $\frac{3}{4}$ of the girls in his school enjoyed reading as a hobby. There are 264 girls in his school. How many girls like to read?
   Ⓐ 198 girls
   Ⓑ 79 girls
   Ⓒ 32 girls
   Ⓓ 238 girls

10. Luis found that the 89 students in his class each spend about $11.18 a month on their hobbies. What is the total amount that these students spend each month on their hobbies?
   Ⓐ $995.02
   Ⓑ $190.06
   Ⓒ $ 99.50
   Ⓓ $877.32

Luis read some interesting facts about animals. Read what Luis learned. Then do Numbers 11 through 14.

BATS

Bats are the only flying mammals. There are over 900 species of bats. About $\frac{1}{5}$ of the mammals in the world are bats. Most bats eat fruit or insects, but some eat lizards, birds, or fish.

CATS

Cats were pets in ancient Egypt, over 3,000 years ago. There are about 36 different species of cats. House cats are the smallest; tigers are the largest. Lions, tigers, leopards, and jaguars are also members of the cat family: they are panthers. Some other cats are cheetahs, pumas, and wildcats.

DOGS

Early humans recognized the dog's excellent senses of hearing and smell and used dogs for hunting, pulling sleds, herding sheep, and protecting other animals and property. Dogs are related to wolves, foxes, and jackals.

---

11. Luis read that the long-eared bat is only 90 millimeters long, and that 44% of that length is its ears. How long are the ears of this bat?

Ⓐ 3,960 mm

Ⓑ   39.6 mm

Ⓒ   396 mm

Ⓓ   3.96 mm

12. Luis wanted to learn more about bats. At a book store, he purchased a book about bats at a price of $8.95, plus 5% sales tax. How much did Luis spend for the book?

Ⓐ $ 8.99

Ⓑ $ 9.39

Ⓒ $ 9.40

Ⓓ $13.43

13. The heaviest dog ever was a Saint Bernard that weighed $140\frac{3}{5}$ kilograms. Luis figured out how much 8 dogs of this size would weigh together. What was his correct total?

Ⓐ 1,124.8 kg

Ⓑ 1,121.2 kg

Ⓒ 1,122.4 kg

Ⓓ 1,126.4 kg

14. Luis read that the smallest cat is the rusty-spotted cat, which weighs $1\frac{2}{5}$ kilograms. He read that the heaviest cat is the Siberian tiger, which weighs 274 times as much. How much does a Siberian tiger weigh?

Ⓐ 465.8 kg

Ⓑ 238.8 kg

Ⓒ 301.4 kg

Ⓓ 383.6 kg

▶ A test question about multiplication may ask for a product when one factor is a decimal, an amount of money, a fraction, a mixed number, or a percent.

▶ A test question about multiplication may ask you to find the total cost of an item, including tax.

Luis read an ad for a Hawaiian vacation. Read this part of the ad. Then do Numbers 15 and 16.

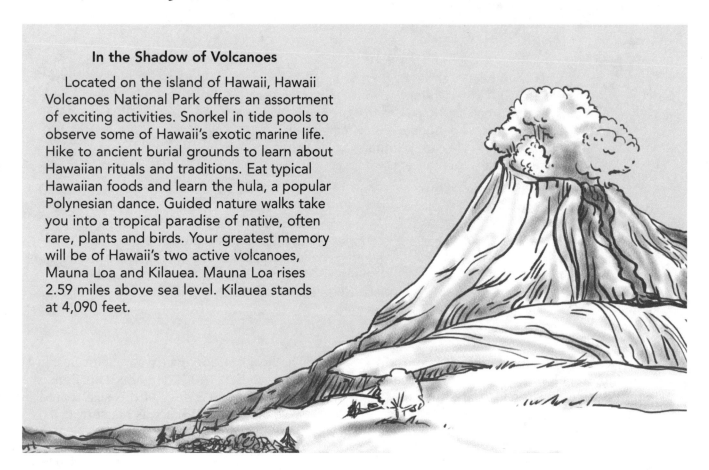

In the Shadow of Volcanoes

Located on the island of Hawaii, Hawaii Volcanoes National Park offers an assortment of exciting activities. Snorkel in tide pools to observe some of Hawaii's exotic marine life. Hike to ancient burial grounds to learn about Hawaiian rituals and traditions. Eat typical Hawaiian foods and learn the hula, a popular Polynesian dance. Guided nature walks take you into a tropical paradise of native, often rare, plants and birds. Your greatest memory will be of Hawaii's two active volcanoes, Mauna Loa and Kilauea. Mauna Loa rises 2.59 miles above sea level. Kilauea stands at 4,090 feet.

Applying Multiplication

15. Luis determined the height of Mauna Lao in feet. Since there are 5,280 feet in a mile, what was his correct solution?
    - Ⓐ 13,675.2 feet
    - Ⓑ   1,368.52 feet
    - Ⓒ 84,449 feet
    - Ⓓ   8,448.8 feet

Applying Multiplication

16. Another Hawaiian volcano, Haleakala, has been dormant since about 1790. Luis read that it is $2\frac{1}{2}$ times the height of Kilauea. What is the height of Haleakala?
    - Ⓐ   8,998 feet
    - Ⓑ 10,225 feet
    - Ⓒ   6,135 feet
    - Ⓓ   8,384.5 feet

Luis found this ad in a magazine called *Kids World*. Read the ad. Then do Numbers 17 and 18.

ATTENTION KIDS!

Do you have a camera? *Kids World* wants YOUR pictures!

Announcing the first annual *Kids World* photography contest!

Send us your color or black-and-white photographs. Judges will choose a first-place winner in each of these four categories: nature/scenic, people, action, animals. One of these will be the grand-prize winner. The grand-prize photograph will be featured on a cover of *Kids World*. The three other first-place photos will appear inside the magazine in a special article about kids and photography. The grand-prize winner will also receive a $1,000 college scholarship. Runners-up will receive *Kids World* T-shirts. The contest will be judged by the editors and writers of *Kids World*.

Send your entry in an envelope, along with a description of the photograph. Tell us where and when you took it, and with what kind of camera. Also, tell us your age and home address. Remember to mark the outside of the envelope with the words "PHOTOS—DO NOT BEND!"

Applying Multiplication

17. Luis bought film to take some photographs for the contest. He bought 6 rolls of film at a price of $5.99 each, plus 5% sales tax. What did he spend for the film?
    - Ⓐ $53.73
    - Ⓑ $21.49
    - Ⓒ $37.74
    - Ⓓ $35.87

Applying Multiplication

18. The magazine received a total of 7,849 photos. Of these, 62% were photographs of animals. How many photos were pictures of animals? Round your answer to the nearest whole number.
    - Ⓐ 4,866 photos
    - Ⓑ 3,431 photos
    - Ⓒ 628 photos
    - Ⓓ 4,870 photos

Strategy Six APPLYING DIVISION

PART ONE: Learn About Division

Study the division problem that Calvin's teacher wrote on the board. As you study, think about the way that Calvin solved it.

Problem: 23,067 ÷ 3,459 (Express your answer to the nearest whole number.)

How Calvin Solves the Problem

I write the problem in long-division form. I am rounding to ones, so I rewrite the dividend one place farther, to tenths, by adding a decimal point and one zero.

I solve for ones; then for tenths.

I write my answer so that the place values of the quotient line up with the place values of the dividend. I write the decimal point in the quotient directly above the decimal point in the dividend.

I round the quotient to the nearest whole number.

round to nearest whole number ⟶ 7

$$
\begin{array}{r}
(6.6) \\
3459\overline{)23067.0} \\
-\ 20754 \\
\hline
23130 \\
-\ 20754 \\
\hline
2376
\end{array}
$$

tenths

Answer: To the nearest whole number, 23,067 ÷ 3,459 = 7.

To express a quotient as the nearest whole percent, solve to thousandths. To express a quotient to the nearest tenth of a percent, solve to ten thousandths, and so on. Convert the quotient to a percentage by multiplying by 100 and adding a percent symbol (%). Round, if necessary.

Example: Lorna had 14 apples. She gave 3 apples to Jim. About what percentage of her apples did Lorna give to Jim? Express your answer to the nearest percent.

Solution: Write problem in long-division form. Solve to thousandths.

Multiply by 100. Add percent symbol.
Round to nearest percent.
0.214 × 100 = 21.4 → 21.4% →21%

$$
\begin{array}{r}
0.214 \\
14\overline{)3.000} \\
-2\,8 \\
\hline
20 \\
-14 \\
\hline
60 \\
56 \\
\hline
4
\end{array}
$$

Answer: Lorna gave about 21% of her apples to Jim.

When solving long division, begin at the dividend digit that has the highest place value. Work from left to right until you reach the dividend digit with the lowest place value.

You use long **division** to find a quotient.

▶ When the dividend cannot be divided evenly by the divisor, add a decimal point and zeros to the dividend. Rewrite the dividend one place farther than the place value you are rounding to.

▶ To express a quotient as a percent, multiply by 100 and add a percent sign.

Study another one of Calvin's problems. Look at the way that Calvin solved the problem. Then do Numbers 1 through 4.

Problem: Janine's parents took turns driving on the way to Denver. The total distance was 2,374 miles. Janine's father drove 1,485 miles. About what percent of the total distance did he drive? Express your answer to the nearest percent.

I write the problem in long-division form. I want to find a percent, so I rewrite the dividend to thousandths.

I solve from left to right. I write the decimal point in the quotient directly above the decimal point in the dividend.

I multiply the quotient by 100 and add the percent symbol.

I round to the nearest percent.

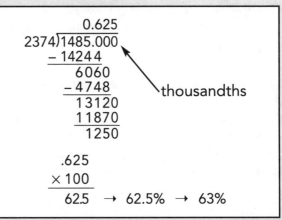

```
        0.625
2374)1485.000
   - 1424 4
       6060
     - 4748          thousandths
      13120
      11870
       1250
```

```
  .625
× 100
  62.5  →  62.5%  →  63%
```

Answer: Janine's father drove about 63% of the total distance.

1. Denver has an area of 153.3 square miles and had a population of 499,055 in 1998. Calvin found the population density of Denver by calculating the number of people per square mile. What was his correct answer, to the nearest whole number?
   - Ⓐ 3,255
   - Ⓒ 3,658
   - Ⓑ 3,072
   - Ⓓ 2,361

2. Calvin read that Denver has about 17,747 acres of public parks. The total area of Denver is 98,112 acres. To the nearest percent, how much of Denver's area is public parks?
   - Ⓐ 6%
   - Ⓒ 2%
   - Ⓑ 18%
   - Ⓓ 34%

3. In 1990, Denver had a population of 467,610. Its population increased by 31,445 from 1990 to 1998. Calvin figured out the percent increase in population by dividing 31,445 by 467,610. What was his correct answer, to the nearest tenth of a percent?
   - Ⓐ 0.1%
   - Ⓒ 67%
   - Ⓑ 6.8%
   - Ⓓ 6.7%

4. Calvin found Denver's average yearly population increase from 1990 to 1998. He divided 31,445 equally over 8 years. To the nearest whole number, what was his correct answer?
   - Ⓐ 2,544
   - Ⓒ 3,931
   - Ⓑ 3,875
   - Ⓓ 4,268

Work with a partner.

Talk about your answers to questions 1–4. Tell why you chose the answers you did.

Remember: You use long division to find a quotient.

▶ When the dividend cannot be divided evenly by the divisor, add a decimal point and zeros to the dividend. Rewrite the dividend one place farther than the place value you are rounding to.

▶ To express a quotient as a percent, multiply by 100 and add a percent sign.

Solve this problem. As you work, ask yourself, "How do I express this quotient as a percent?"

5. Calvin learned that Colorado has 250 peaks that are over 13,000 feet. Of these peaks, 53 are over 14,000 feet. What percentage of the 250 peaks are over 14,000 feet high? Express your answer to the nearest percent.
   Ⓐ 21%
   Ⓑ 5%
   Ⓒ 2%
   Ⓓ 22%

Solve another problem. As you work, ask yourself, "How do I use zeros and a decimal point to find the quotient?"

6. In 1998, Colorado had a population of 3,970,971, and produced nonfuel minerals valued at $604,000,000. What was Calvin's correct finding of this amount per person? Express your answer to the nearest dollar.
   Ⓐ $1,521
   Ⓑ $ 153
   Ⓒ $ 152
   Ⓓ $ 150

Look at the answer choices for each question.
Read why each answer choice is correct or not correct.

5. Calvin learned that Colorado has 250 peaks that are over 13,000 feet. Of these peaks, 53 are over 14,000 feet. What percentage of the 250 peaks are over 14,000 feet high? Express your answer to the nearest percent.

● 21%

This answer is correct because you must solve 53.000 ÷ 250, to thousandths; multiply the quotient, 0.212, by 100; and add the percent symbol, to get 21.2%, or, to the nearest percent, 21%.

Ⓑ 5%

This answer is not correct because you must first solve 53.000 ÷ 250, to thousandths. Maybe you solved 250 ÷ 53 to the nearest percent, and did not multiply by 100.

Ⓒ 2%

This answer is not correct because after you solve 53.000 ÷ 250, to thousandths, you multiply the quotient, 0.212, by 100. Maybe you multiplied by 10, and rounded to the nearest percent.

Ⓓ 22%

This answer is not correct because after you solve 53.000 ÷ 250, to thousandths; multiply the quotient, 0.212, by 100; and add the percent symbol; to get 21.2%, you round down to the nearest percent, 21%. Maybe you rounded up.

6. In 1998, Colorado had a population of 3,970,971, and produced nonfuel minerals valued at $604,000,000. What was Calvin's correct finding of this amount per person? Express your answer to the nearest dollar.

Ⓐ $1,521

This answer is not correct because you must solve $604,000,000.0 ÷ 3,970,971, which is $152.1, or, to the nearest dollar, is $152. Maybe you added the decimal point and zero to the dividend but forgot the decimal point in the quotient.

Ⓑ $153

This answer is not correct because you must solve $604,000,000.0 ÷ 3,970,971, which is $152.1, or, to the nearest dollar, is $152, not $153.

● $152

This answer is correct because you must solve $604,000,000.0 ÷ 3,970,971, which is $152.1, or, to the nearest dollar, is $152.

Ⓓ $150

This answer is not correct because you must solve $604,000,000.0 ÷ 3,970,971, which is $152.1, or, to the nearest dollar, is $152, not $150.

Sometimes, a dividend cannot be divided equally by the divisor. When this happens, the quotient will have a remainder.

▶ Use long division to solve the problem. Solve only to ones.

▶ The remainder is the number that is left over after solving for the ones digit and subtracting. The remainder must be less than the divisor.

▶ To check the answer, multiply the divisor by the quotient, and then add the remainder to the product. The total equals the dividend.

▶ To round a quotient with a remainder, follow this rule: If the remainder is one-half or more than the divisor, round up the quotient to the next whole number. If the remainder is less than one-half the divisor, do not round up.

Problem: $643 \div 14$

1. Solve with long division. Divide the tens. Multiply and subtract. Bring down the ones digit. Divide the ones. Multiply and subtract.	2. Write the remainder.	3. Check the answer.
$\begin{array}{r} 45 \\ 14\overline{)643} \\ -56 \\ \hline 83 \\ -70 \\ \hline 13 \end{array}$	$\begin{array}{r} 45 \\ 14\overline{)643} \\ -56 \\ \hline 83 \\ -70 \\ \hline (13) \end{array}$ ← remainder → $\begin{array}{r} 45\ R13 \\ 14\overline{)643} \end{array}$	$\begin{array}{r} 14 \\ \times 45 \\ \hline 630 \end{array}$ $\begin{array}{r} 630 \\ + 13 \\ \hline 643 \end{array}$

Answer: $643 \div 14 = 45\ R13$

Calvin did some research about Colorado. Do Numbers 7 through 10.

7. Colorado had a 1998 population of 3,970,971 living in 63 counties. If each county had an equal population, what would be the population of each, and how many people would be left over?
   - Ⓐ 63,031 R18
   - Ⓑ 63,031 R29
   - Ⓒ 63,047 R34
   - Ⓓ 62,984 R7

8. Colorado has 24,137,000 acres of forests, and, in 1998, Colorado produced 114,000,000 feet of lumber. How many feet is that per acre of forest? Round to the nearest foot.
   - Ⓐ 7 ft
   - Ⓑ 4 ft
   - Ⓒ 5 ft
   - Ⓓ 9 ft

9. Colorado had 29,500 farms and 3.1 million cattle in 1998. If the cattle were distributed equally, how many would there be on each farm, and how many would be left over?
   - Ⓐ 1,051 R4
   - Ⓑ 105 R2,500
   - Ⓒ 110 R84
   - Ⓓ 85 R12,250

10. Colorado's 29,500 farms cover 32,200,000 acres of farmland. If each farm were the same size, how many acres would each farm be? Round to the nearest acre.
    - Ⓐ 1,167 acres
    - Ⓑ 916 acres
    - Ⓒ 1,090 acres
    - Ⓓ 1,092 acres

Calvin wrote a report about Native Americans. Read this part of his report. Then do Numbers 11 through 14.

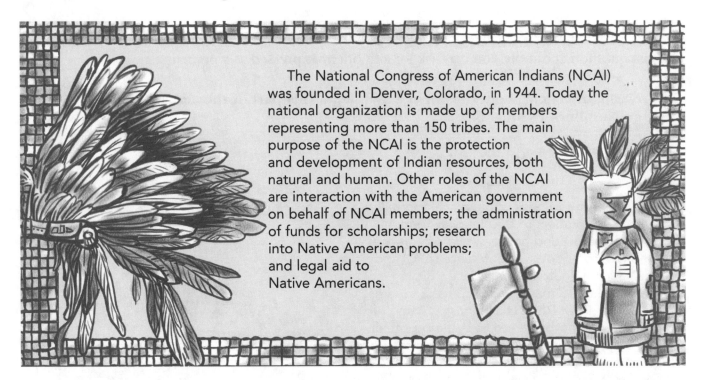

The National Congress of American Indians (NCAI) was founded in Denver, Colorado, in 1944. Today the national organization is made up of members representing more than 150 tribes. The main purpose of the NCAI is the protection and development of Indian resources, both natural and human. Other roles of the NCAI are interaction with the American government on behalf of NCAI members; the administration of funds for scholarships; research into Native American problems; and legal aid to Native Americans.

11. In the 1990s, 155 tribes, representing 600,000 Native Americans, were members of the NCAI. If there were an equal number of Native Americans in each member tribe, how many would be in each tribe, and how many would be left over?

Ⓐ 2,583 R33

Ⓑ 3,870 R150

Ⓒ 3,870 R97

Ⓓ 4,019 R6

12. In 1990, there were 1,959,234 Native Americans in the U.S., and 949,075 lived on or near federal reservations. To the nearest percent, what part of the Native American population was living on or near reservations?

Ⓐ 49%

Ⓑ 52%

Ⓒ 5%

Ⓓ 48%

13. In 1990, 949,075 Native Americans lived on or near 287 federal reservations. If their population were divided equally among the 287 reservations, how many Native Americans would live on or near each reservation? Round to the nearest whole number.

Ⓐ 3,307

Ⓑ 3,023

Ⓒ 3,500

Ⓓ 3,416

14. In 1990, 54,400,000 acres of land were held in trust by the federal government for 1,959,234 Native Americans. To the nearest tenth of an acre, how much land is that per Native American?

Ⓐ 27.8 acres

Ⓑ 3.6 acres

Ⓒ 27.7 acres

Ⓓ 306.4 acres

▶ A test question about division may require you to rewrite a dividend, by adding a decimal point and zeros, in order to find a quotient when the dividend cannot be evenly divided by the divisor.

▶ A test question about division may ask for a quotient that has a remainder.

▶ A test question about division may ask for a quotient expressed as a percent.

Calvin read an article about the Super Bowl. Read this part of the article. Then do Numbers 15 and 16.

The Super Bowl

In the United States, professional football teams, all members of the National Football League, are divided between two conferences: the American Football Conference (AFC) and the National Football Conference (NFC). The AFC has 16 teams and NFC has 15 teams. The Super Bowl is the championship game of professional football. Each year, the best team from each conference plays each other in a game in January, after the regular season has ended. The first Super Bowl was held in 1967. Each year, the Super Bowl is the most-watched sports event in the world. In fact, as of 1999, 19 Super Bowls were in the top 45 most-watched television programs of all time!

Applying Division

15. As of January 1999, the Pittsburgh Steelers had played in 5 Super Bowls and won 4. In those 5 games, 220 total points were scored by Pittsburgh and the opposing teams. Pittsburgh scored 120 points. What percent of the total points was scored by Pittsburgh? Round to the nearest percent.

    Ⓐ 38%
    Ⓑ 55%
    Ⓒ 28%
    Ⓓ 54%

Applying Division

16. Through 1999, the Dallas Cowboys played in 8 Super Bowls, more than any other team. They scored a total of 221 points in those 8 games. What was their average Super Bowl score per game? Round to the nearest point.

    Ⓐ 29 points
    Ⓑ 35 points
    Ⓒ 23 points
    Ⓓ 28 points

Calvin wrote this journal entry. Read the entry. Then do Numbers 17 and 18.

September 16

Yesterday was my football team's first game of the season. We have been practicing twice a week for the last 4 weeks, and that has really paid off! We won! My team, the Springfield Serpents, beat the Lincoln Lions, 32 to 13! I even scored a touchdown. When I woke up yesterday and saw that it was raining, I was worried that our game would be canceled. But our coach told us that football games are played in rain, snow, and other bad weather. Everyone was upset about the rain at first, but then we found out how much fun it was. It was really messy! The rain-soaked field was covered with patches of slippery, wet grass and sloppy mud puddles. Our white uniforms were mostly brown by the end of the game. Next week's game is against the Cooperville Cougars. Coach Thompson says they are a strong team, so we will have to practice hard this week if we want to beat them. I know we will!

Applying Division

17. The parents of Calvin's teammates brought water to the game. They brought 12 gallons of water for the 18 players. To the nearest hundredth of a gallon, how much water was there for each player?

    Ⓐ 1.50 gal
    Ⓑ 0.67 gal
    Ⓒ 2.16 gal
    Ⓓ 0.66 gal

Applying Division

18. The game between the Lions and the Serpents was attended by 455 people. The bleachers became full, so some people had to stand. If 50 people sat in each row of the bleachers, how many people had to stand?

    Ⓐ   5 people
    Ⓑ   9 people
    Ⓒ 50 people
    Ⓓ   3 people

PART ONE: Read a Story

Read the story. Then do Numbers 1 through 6.

June 12, 1997

Dear Friend,

Hello. My name is Kathy MacNeal. I am 11 years old, and I live in New Jersey, USA. I am putting this message in a bottle and dropping the bottle into the ocean. If you find it, maybe we could be e-mail pen pals! If you want to, you can write to me at KathyMac@superdupermail.com, and I will write back. Bye!

Kathy folded the note and placed it inside a clean, empty soda bottle. She screwed on the cap and dropped the bottle off the pier. She turned and walked away, wondering if anyone would ever find her note.

August 14, 1999

Kathy sat at the computer to check her e-mail. There were six messages. She figured they were from the usual mix of friends and family. As she scanned her "In" box, she saw an e-mail address she didn't recognize. The subject of the e-mail was "Message in a Bottle." Kathy excitedly recalled the bottle she'd dropped into the ocean two years earlier. She had learned at school not to open e-mail from strangers, so she called her mom in to check it. Her mom quickly read the note, and then smiled and told Kathy to read it.

TO: KathyMac@superdupermail.com	FROM: LiamOMalley@free-e-post.uk
SUBJECT: Message in a Bottle	DATE: August 14, 1999

Dear Kathy,

While walking on the beach yesterday, I found your bottle and read your message. My name is Liam O'Malley, and I am 14 years old. I live in Ireland. Your bottle has traveled all the way across the Atlantic Ocean! I would love to be pen pals. Write back, and tell me about yourself. What do you like to do? Do you play any sports?

Best wishes,
Liam

P.S.: When did you drop the bottle in the ocean? I am wondering how long it took to reach me.

Applying Subtraction

1. Kathy and her parents planned a trip to Ireland. They found a round-trip airfare of $589.50 per person, and a bargain airfare of $379.95 per person. How much less is the bargain airfare?
   - Ⓐ $210.65
   - Ⓑ $210.45
   - Ⓒ $220.55
   - Ⓓ $209.55

Applying Multiplication

4. Kathy calculated the cost for 4 adults to fly to Ireland at the bargain airfare of $379.95 per person. What was her correct total?
   - Ⓐ $1,286.60
   - Ⓑ $1,519.80
   - Ⓒ $1,508.70
   - Ⓓ $1,206.80

Applying Subtraction

2. Liam's house is $4\frac{1}{2}$ miles from the ocean. Kathy lives $63\frac{3}{8}$ miles from the ocean. How many miles closer to the ocean is Liam's house?
   - Ⓐ $59\frac{1}{8}$ miles
   - Ⓑ $58\frac{7}{8}$ miles
   - Ⓒ $57\frac{1}{2}$ miles
   - Ⓓ $60\frac{1}{3}$ miles

Applying Division

5. In their first year as pen pals, Kathy and Liam exchanged a total of 682 e-mail messages. Kathy wrote 311 of those messages. What percentage of the messages did Kathy write? Round your answer to the nearest percent.
   - Ⓐ 46%
   - Ⓑ 22%
   - Ⓒ 45%
   - Ⓓ 54%

Applying Multiplication

3. Kathy bought a book about Ireland. The price of the book was $11.95, plus 6% sales tax. What did she spend for the book? Round your answer to the nearest cent.
   - Ⓐ $12.71
   - Ⓑ $19.12
   - Ⓒ $12.67
   - Ⓓ $12.15

Applying Division

6. Kathy and Liam figured out that the bottle traveled 3,392 miles in 793 days. To the nearest hundredth, how many miles is that per day?
   - Ⓐ 26.89 mi
   - Ⓑ 0.23 mi
   - Ⓒ 4.30 mi
   - Ⓓ 4.28 mi

Here is a summary of a nonfiction book. Read the summary. Then do Numbers 7 through 12.

Shipwreck at the Bottom of the World, by Jennifer Armstrong, tells the fascinating true story of Ernest Shackleton and the Imperial Trans-Antarctic Expedition. Shackleton led the expedition in an attempt to become the first explorer to cross Antarctica.

In August of 1914, Shackleton sailed from England with a 27-man team aboard his ship, *Endurance.* His team included sailors and scientists. There were two surgeons, a biologist, a meteorologist, a geologist, and a physicist. He also brought an artist, a photographer, a carpenter, a cook, and two firemen. There was even one stowaway! A man named Percy Blackborrow, helped by another sailor on the ship, came aboard during a stop in Argentina and then hid in a locker until the ship was at sea for three days. When Blackborrow emerged, Shackleton—called "the boss" by his crew—was amused by the young man and gave him a position on the ship.

After sailing for five months, *Endurance* became trapped in ice about 100 miles from land. The expedition team remained on the ice-bound ship throughout the frigid Antarctic winter. Then, in the spring, large pieces of ice, called floes, began moving and pressing into the sides of the ship. Eventually, the floes crushed the ship, and it sank.

The boss and his team had removed the ship's lifeboats, equipment, and supplies. At first, they attempted to haul their supplies to Paulet Island, where there would be food and shelter, even though it would be a 346-mile trek, under terrible conditions. After two days, they'd moved only about two miles. They found themselves on a large, solid, flat ice floe and made camp. For another five months, the team camped while the floe drifted northward, carrying them closer to Paulet Island. Eventually, the floe began to melt. Shackleton decided they would sail in the lifeboats to Elephant Island, where they hoped to find help.

After a long, treacherous journey, they reached Elephant Island. But the only hope for Shackleton's men was a rescue party. With five men, the boss sailed a 20-foot lifeboat across 800 miles of dangerous ocean to South Georgia Island. When they landed, three of the men were so sick that they stayed in the shelter of a cave. The boss and the other two men hiked across the icy, treacherous interior of the island, crossing mountains and glaciers, until they reached a whaling station. The three men in the cave were retrieved and brought to the whaling station. It was four months before conditions allowed Shackleton and a rescue party to sail to Elephant Island.

In August 1916, the rescuers reached the camp on Elephant Island. After nineteen months trapped in the icy Antarctic, Shackleton brought every one of his men home alive.

ANTARCTICA

Applying Subtraction

7. Antarctica's highest mountain is Vinson Massif, at 16,860.24 feet. The highest peak in the world, Mt. Everest, is 29,022.31 feet. How much higher is Mt. Everest?

Ⓐ 12,162.07 feet

Ⓑ 13,842.13 feet

Ⓒ 13,262.17 feet

Ⓓ 11,242.04 feet

Applying Multiplication

10. The U.S. is about 29% of the area of Antarctica's ice sheet. If the ice sheet is 13 million square miles, how big is the U.S.? Round your answer to the nearest tenth of a million.

Ⓐ 37.7 million square miles

Ⓑ 4.5 million square miles

Ⓒ 3.8 million square miles

Ⓓ 2.2 million square miles

Applying Subtraction

8. The longest glacier in the world, the Lambert/Fisher Ice Passage in Antarctica, is $320\frac{1}{10}$ miles long. The second longest, the Novaya Zemlya Glacier in Russia, is $259\frac{4}{5}$ miles long. How much longer is the Antarctic glacier?

Ⓐ $40\frac{3}{10}$ miles

Ⓑ $139\frac{1}{2}$ miles

Ⓒ $61\frac{3}{5}$ miles

Ⓓ $60\frac{3}{10}$ miles

Applying Division

11. The first successful Trans-Antarctic crossing was completed in 1958. A team, led by Dr. Vivian E. Fuchs, crossed 2,158 miles in 98 days. How many miles would that be per day, and how many would be left over?

Ⓐ 22 R2

Ⓑ 21 R21

Ⓒ 23 R92

Ⓓ 20 R12

Applying Multiplication

9. *Endurance* was 43.89 meters long and 7.62 meters wide. If the ship were a rectangle, what would its area be? Round your answer to the nearest hundredth.

Ⓐ 333.64 square meters

Ⓑ 657.95 square meters

Ⓒ 334.44 square meters

Ⓓ 307.36 square meters

Applying Division

12. In 1997, Borge Ousland became the first person to cross Antarctica alone. His journey of 1,675 miles took 64 days. To the nearest mile, how far is that per day?

Ⓐ 38 miles

Ⓑ 27 miles

Ⓒ 16 miles

Ⓓ 26 miles

Strategy Seven CONVERTING TIME AND MONEY

PART ONE: Learn About Time

Study the problem that LuAn solved. As you study, think about how LuAn solved it.

Problem: A woman has a meeting at 5:45 P.M. She leaves home at the time shown. The woman hopes to get to the meeting ½ hour early to take care of other business, but traffic is heavy, and the drive takes her 78 minutes. What time does the woman get to her meeting? Considering the traffic, what time should she have left home to get to her meeting ½ hour early?

How LuAn Solves the Problem

1. To find what time the woman gets to her meeting, I convert 78 minutes to 1 hour, 18 minutes; and I add times.
   - I add the minutes first. Then I add hours. I see that 70 is greater than 60, so I regroup 60 minutes as 1 hour.
   - I could also count on from 4:52 on the clock face, counting up 1 hour, 18 minutes to 6:10 P.M.

$$
\begin{array}{r}
1 \\
4\text{ h }52\text{ min} \\
+\ 1\text{ h }18\text{ min} \\
\hline
5\text{ h }70\text{ min} = \\
6\text{ h }10\text{ min}
\end{array}
$$

2. To find what time the woman should have left home, I add 30 minutes (½ hour) to 78 minutes to get 108 minutes, or 1 hour, 48 minutes. Then I subtract.
   - I look at the minutes. I see that 48 is greater than 45, so I regroup 1 hour as 60 minutes. I add 60 to 45 to get 105. I subtract hours and minutes and get 3 hours, 57 minutes.
   - I could also count back 1 hour, 48 minutes on a clock face.

hours	minutes
4	105
5̶:	4̶5̶
− 1:	48
3:	57

Answer: The woman arrives at the meeting at 6:10 P.M. She should have left home at 3:57 P.M.

You can tell how much **time** has passed or remains between events.

▶ Use a clock face to count on or count back; or, use addition or subtraction.

▶ To add times together, first add the minutes, then add the hours, regrouping 60 minutes to 1 hour, if necessary.

▶ To subtract times, first subtract the minutes, regrouping 1 hour to 60 minutes, if necessary. Then subtract the hours.

▶ Use time facts to find how many minutes, hours, fractions of an hour, days, weeks, and so on, have passed or remain.

Study another one of LuAn's problems. Look at how LuAn solved the problem. Then do Numbers 1 through 4.

Problem: Two students are at an all-day conference on school government. They plan to meet for lunch after the morning sessions. They attend different sessions that start at the same time. The girl's session lasts $\frac{3}{4}$ hour. The boy's session lasts $1\frac{1}{4}$ hours. How long does the girl have to wait for the boy?

I know there are 60 minutes in 1 hour.	
I multiply $\frac{3}{4}$ times 60 and get 45 minutes.	$\frac{3}{4} \times \frac{\overset{15}{\cancel{60}}}{1} = 45$ min
I multiply $1\frac{1}{4}$ times 60 and get 75 minutes.	$\frac{5}{4} \times \frac{\overset{15}{\cancel{60}}}{1} = 75$ min
I subtract 45 minutes from 75 minutes to get 30 minutes.	75 min − 45 min = 30 min
I know that 60 divided by 30 is 2, so I know that 30 minutes is $\frac{1}{2}$ of 60, or $\frac{1}{2}$ hour.	30 min = $\frac{1}{2}$ hour

Answer: The girl has to wait 30 minutes, or $\frac{1}{2}$ hour for the boy.

1. LuAn was sick and had to stay in bed. When she began to feel better, she figured out that she had not been out of her room for 259,200 seconds. What time period is equal to 259,200 seconds?
   - Ⓐ 3 hours
   - Ⓑ 3 days
   - Ⓒ 3 weeks
   - Ⓓ 3 months

2. On Monday, LuAn arrived at the doctor's office at the time shown. She had to wait 33 minutes to see the doctor. What time did LuAn see the doctor?

   - Ⓐ 1:27 P.M.
   - Ⓑ 1:21 P.M.
   - Ⓒ 12:37 P.M.
   - Ⓓ 12:57 P.M.

3. LuAn's friend Inez came to visit for $3\frac{1}{2}$ hours on Friday. The girls spent $\frac{3}{4}$ hour talking; then they went for a short walk that took $\frac{1}{3}$ hour. The rest of the time they played a board game. How much time did they spend playing the game?
   - Ⓐ 1 hour, 20 minutes
   - Ⓑ 1 hour, 15 minutes
   - Ⓒ 2 hours, 5 minutes
   - Ⓓ 2 hours, 25 minutes

4. Inez brought LuAn's homework to her. Inez left LuAn's at the time shown. LuAn wanted to see a show at 8:00 P.M. How much time remained for LuAn to finish her homework?
   - Ⓐ 2 hours, 21 minutes
   - Ⓑ 2 hours, 19 minutes
   - Ⓒ 1 hour, 41 minutes
   - Ⓓ 1 hour, 11 minutes

Talk about your answers to questions 1–4. Tell why you chose the answers you did.

Remember: You can tell how much time has passed or remains between events.

▶ Use a clock face to count on or count back; or, use addition or subtraction.

▶ To add times together, first add the minutes, then add the hours, regrouping 60 minutes to 1 hour, if necessary.

▶ To subtract times, first subtract the minutes, regrouping 1 hour to 60 minutes, if necessary. Then subtract the hours.

▶ Use time facts to find how many minutes, hours, fractions of an hour, days, weeks, and so on, have passed or remain.

Solve this problem. As you work, ask yourself, "Can I use a clock face to count back? Can I use addition or subtraction to find the time?"

5. In the morning, LuAn is scheduled to deliver a talk at a speech competition at the time shown. She wants to practice for at least $2\frac{1}{3}$ hours before she speaks. What time should she start to practice her speech?

ⓐ 10:05 A.M.

ⓑ 9:40 A.M.

ⓒ 10:30 A.M.

ⓓ 9:50 A.M.

Solve another problem. As you work, ask yourself, "How can I convert minutes to hours to find how much time has passed?"

6. Each speech in the competition must be at least 18 minutes long but no longer than 24 minutes. Twelve students speak the minimum amount of time and speak for 216 minutes all together. Eight students speak the maximum amount of time and speak for 192 minutes all together. With a 1-hour break for lunch, how long will the competition last?

ⓐ $6\frac{3}{4}$ hours

ⓑ $7\frac{4}{5}$ hours

ⓒ $19\frac{1}{2}$ hours

ⓓ $6\frac{4}{5}$ hours

Look at the answer choices for each question.
Read why each answer choice is correct or not correct.

5. In the morning, LuAn is scheduled to deliver a talk at a speech competition at the time shown. She wants to practice for at least $2\frac{1}{3}$ hours before she speaks. What time should she start to practice her speech?

Ⓐ 10:05 A.M.

This answer is not correct because if you count back from 12:10 on a clock face 2 hours and 20 minutes, you get to 9:50.

Ⓑ 9:40 A.M.

This answer is not correct because it is too early. You may not have converted $2\frac{1}{3}$ hours correctly to 2 hours, 20 minutes before subtracting from 12:10.

Ⓒ 10:30 A.M.

This answer is not correct because it is too late. If you subtract 2 hours, 20 minutes from 12:10, you get 9:50.

● 9:50 A.M.

This answer is correct because $2\frac{1}{3}$ hours converts to 2 hours, 20 minutes, and that time subtracted from 12:10 is 9:50.

6. Each speech in the competition must be at least 18 minutes long but no longer than 24 minutes. Twelve students speak the minimum amount of time and speak for 216 minutes all together. Eight students speak the maximum amount of time and speak for 192 minutes all together. With a 1-hour break for lunch, how long will the competition last?

Ⓐ $6\frac{3}{4}$ hours

This answer is not correct because it is less than the actual amount of time. You may not have converted minutes to hours correctly.

● $7\frac{4}{5}$ hours

This answer is correct because if you convert 1 hour to 60 minutes and add it to the minutes given, you get 468 minutes, which equals 7 hours, 48 minutes, or $7\frac{4}{5}$ hours.

Ⓒ $19\frac{1}{2}$ hours

This answer is not correct because it is more than the actual amount of time. There are 60 minutes in an hour so $468 \div 60 = 7\frac{4}{5}$ hours.

Ⓓ $6\frac{4}{5}$ hours

This answer is not correct because it is less than the actual amount of time. You may not have added the 60 minute lunch break.

You can use what you know about time to figure how long a job will take. You can use what you know about the value of bills and coins to count **money**.

▶ When you want to know how long a job will take and are given the time it takes to do an individual task, figure out how many times you have to repeat the task. Then multiply that number by the time given.

> It takes 9 minutes, 15 seconds to run around the block 3 times. To figure out how long it takes to run around the block 15 times, divide 15 by 3 to get 5. Next, multiply 5 × 9 minutes, 15 seconds and get 45 minutes, 75 seconds, which equals 46 minutes, 15 seconds.

▶ When you want to know the total value of a group of bills or coins, count all of one denomination before going on to the next lowest denomination of bill or coin.

▶ To find how many coins are in a dollar value, multiply by the number of coins in $1.00. For example, to find how many quarters are in $250.00, multiply 250 by 4 (4 quarters = $1.00): $250 × 4 = 1,000 quarters.

▶ To find the dollar value of coins, divide by the number of coins in $1.00. For example, to find the dollar value of 300 nickels, divide by 20. (20 nickels = $1.00): 300 ÷ 20 = $15.00.

LuAn wants to take drum lessons. Do Numbers 7 through 10.

7. LuAn's parents agreed to let her take drum lessons if she pays for half the cost of 6 months' worth of lessons in advance. She needs $396.50. LuAn counted the coins in her bank. She has 1,368 quarters and 93 dimes. Which statement is true?
   Ⓐ LuAn has exactly $396.50.
   Ⓑ LuAn has $10.30 more than she needs.
   Ⓒ LuAn needs $45.20 more.
   Ⓓ LuAn needs 5 more quarters and 2 dimes.

8. Lessons are 35 minutes long. If LuAn takes 4 lessons a month, how much time will she spend on lessons over the next 6 months?
   Ⓐ 56 hours
   Ⓑ 24 hours
   Ⓒ 14 hours
   Ⓓ 35 hours

9. All of LuAn's quarters and dimes are tips she received from customers in her parents' restaurant, where she helps out. On Saturday, after the restaurant closed, LuAn counted the bills in the register, as shown in the chart. What dollar amount do the bills represent?

Denomination	No. of bills
$50	22
$20	229
$10	318
$ 5	231
$ 1	671

   Ⓐ $ 9,832   Ⓒ $10,686
   Ⓑ $11,542   Ⓓ $12,725

10. LuAn will rent a set of drums. The 6-month rental fee is $379.32. If she pays in 20-dollar bills, how many will she need to pay the whole bill?
   Ⓐ 37 bills   Ⓒ 18 bills
   Ⓑ 28 bills   Ⓓ 19 bills

Read the journal entry that LuAn wrote. Then do Numbers 11 through 14.

Saturday, May 10

I'm so tired I can hardly keep my eyes open. I spent the whole day at the restaurant. Usually, I just serve customers and then clean their tables when they leave. But the flu is going around, and one of the waitstaff and two of the cooks didn't show up. Neither did Kim, the cashier. Kim handles all the take-out business. She answers the phone and takes down customers' orders. I didn't understand until today just how hectic her job can be. Dad asked me to be cashier during lunch, since he had to be in the kitchen. Mother was helping the waitstaff in the main dining room. The phone rang constantly for take-outs; meanwhile, customers lined up, waiting to pay. Everyone was very patient with me, but I was glad when the lunch rush was over. It seemed as if I had just caught my breath when Dad told me to get ready for the dinner rush. I'll write about that tomorrow. Now, I'm going to sleep.

11. During the lunch and dinner rush, LuAn answered the phone and wrote down take-out orders. There were 72 calls. Each call averaged 4 minutes, 15 seconds. How much time altogether did LuAn spend taking these orders?

Ⓐ 6 hours, 56 minutes

Ⓑ 5 hours, 6 minutes

Ⓒ 5 hours, 18 minutes

Ⓓ 4 hours, 48 minutes

12. The bill for one large take-out order was $451.67. The man who picked up the order paid in 20-dollar bills. How many bills did he give LuAn if he got $8.33 in change?

Ⓐ 45 bills

Ⓑ 23 bills

Ⓒ 8 bills

Ⓓ 31 bills

13. LuAn put coins from the register into a bank sack. There were 15 golden dollars, 78 half-dollars, 485 quarters, 62 dimes, 95 nickels, and 315 pennies. After lunch, LuAn's mother took the coins to the bank to deposit into the business account. How much were the coins worth?

Ⓐ $319.85

Ⓑ $281

Ⓒ $168.25

Ⓓ $189.35

14. LuAn's dad paid her $6.50 an hour for 9 hours of work over the weekend. Which of these is true?

Ⓐ LuAn's pay equals 234 quarters.

Ⓑ LuAn earned more than the value of three 20-dollar bills.

Ⓒ LuAn earned less than $50.00.

Ⓓ LuAn's pay equals 650 nickels.

▶ A test question about time may ask how much time has passed or remains.

▶ A test question about time may ask you to add or subtract times.

▶ A test question about time may ask you to convert units of time.

▶ A test question about money may ask for the total value of a group of bills or coins.

▶ A test question about money may ask you to convert dollar values to coins or coins to dollar values.

Read why LuAn wanted to play the drums. Then do Numbers 15 and 16.

The Beat Goes On

When LuAn decided that she wanted to play the drums, her parents were happy that she wanted to play an instrument but a little disappointed that she hadn't chosen the violin or the cello or the piano. Those are the instruments that LuAn's mother, father, and brother play. Her parents and brother prefer the classical music of Mozart and Beethoven, whereas LuAn prefers the sounds of American jazz. LuAn is so enthusiastic about jazz that her parents and brother learned a few songs so that they could all play together on family music nights.

Converting Time and Money

15. LuAn's family plays together Thursday and Sunday evenings. Last Sunday, starting at the time shown, they played for $2\frac{3}{4}$ hours. What time did they stop playing?

- Ⓐ 8:52 P.M.
- Ⓒ 9:07 P.M.
- Ⓑ 8:47 P.M.
- Ⓓ 10:15 P.M.

Converting Time and Money

16. LuAn's family enjoys this music game: One person hums the first few notes of a tune; the others have to guess the song; whoever doesn't know the song has to put coins into the family bank. As of last week, there were 43 quarters, 52 dimes, 88 nickels, and 76 pennies in the bank. What is the value of these coins?
- Ⓐ $21.11
- Ⓑ $19.00
- Ⓒ $45.21
- Ⓓ $96.35

Read part of a report that LuAn wrote about jazz. Then do Numbers 17 and 18.

Real American Music

Jazz—which includes ragtime, blues, and swing—was first heard in the late 1800s in the South, but no one is sure exactly where jazz began. Some people say that jazz was born in New Orleans, Louisiana, which is sometimes called the "cradle of jazz."

Jazz started as the folk music of African-Americans. It combined the rhythms of West Africa with the sounds of gospel music, spirituals, and chants sung by enslaved African-Americans. As jazz grew more popular, it spread north to Chicago and New York City, which became centers of jazz. The 1920s were known as the Jazz Age.

Converting Time and Money

17. To prepare her report, LuAn read books and articles about jazz. She also listened to 9 different jazz CDs that she borrowed from the library's audio collection. LuAn noted the playing time of each CD and calculated that it would take an average of 57 minutes to listen to each of the 9 CDs. About how long will it take her to listen to all 9 CDs?

Ⓐ 8 hours, 57 minutes
Ⓑ 7 hours, 59 minutes
Ⓒ 6 hours, 13 minutes
Ⓓ 8 hours, 33 minutes

Converting Time and Money

18. The day after she turned in her report, LuAn auditioned for a summer jazz camp. Three days later, she found out that she had been accepted. She also learned that she had been awarded a tuition scholarship. The tuition for the two-week camp is usually $1,255. Which of these equals $1,255?

Ⓐ 2,510 dimes
Ⓑ 6,275 nickels
Ⓒ 5,020 quarters
Ⓓ 12,550 pennies

Strategy Eight CONVERTING CUSTOMARY AND METRIC MEASURES

PART ONE: Learn About Customary and Metric Measures

Study the problem that Leon's teacher wrote on the board. As you study, think about the way that Leon solved it.

Problem: The highest point in Ohio is Campbell Hill, in Bellefontaine. Campbell Hill is 1,550 feet tall. How many meters represent the same height?
1 foot ≈ 0.3048 meter

How Leon Solves the Problem	
I write the problem.	1,550 ft ≈ _?_ m
I rewrite the problem as a multiplication equation.	1,550 × (1 ft) ≈ _?_ m
I replace 1 foot with its equivalency: 0.3048 meter.	1,550 × (0.3048 m) ≈ _?_ m
I solve 1,550 × 0.3048.	472.44 m ≈ _?_ m
I write the answer.	1,550 ft ≈ 472.44 m

Answer: The height of Campbell Hill is 472.44 meters.

An equivalency is an equal relationship between two units of measurement. An equivalency usually tells the amount of a unit that is equal (=) or approximately equal (≈) to 1 of another unit. For example, 1 ounce = 28 grams is an equivalency that tells you 28 grams are equal to 1 ounce, and 1 mile ≈ 1.609 kilometers is an equivalency that tells you that 1 mile is approximately equal to 1.609 kilometers.

Sometimes, you will need to use division to solve a conversion problem.

Example: Mount Hood, in Oregon, is 11,239 feet tall. What is Mt. Hood's height in meters? Round your answer to the nearest hundredth. (1 meter ≈ 3.281 feet)

Solution:		
	Write the problem.	11,239 ft ≈ _?_ m
	Rewrite the problem.	11,239 ft ≈ _?_ × (1 m)
	Rewrite the problem as a division equation.	11,239 ft ÷ 1 m ≈ _?_
	Replace 1 meter with 3.281 feet.	11,239 ft ÷ 3.281 ft ≈ _?_
	Solve 11,239 ÷ 3.281 to thousandths.	3,425.480 ≈ _?_
	Round to hundredths.	3,425.48 ≈ _?_
	Write the answer.	11,239 ft ≈ 3,425.48 m

You use **conversion** to change a measurement from one unit to another unit.

▶ Rewrite conversion problems as division or multiplication equations.

▶ Use equivalencies to solve conversion equations.

Leon and his classmates measured things in their classroom. Study the chart they made of their measurements. Think about ways to convert measurements from one unit to another. Then do Numbers 1 through 4.

Door (height)	Window (width)	Board (length)	Math Book (weight)	Fish Tank (capacity)
7 feet	48 inches	4 meters	980 grams	11 gallons

1. Leon found that the math book weighed 980 grams. What is the weight of the math book in ounces?

1 gram ≈ 0.035 ounce

Ⓐ 280.0 ounces

Ⓑ 34.3 ounces

Ⓒ 945.96 ounces

Ⓓ 4.9 ounces

2. The fish tank in Leon's classroom holds 11 gallons of water. How many liters of water can the tank hold? Round your answer to the nearest hundredth.

1 gallon ≈ 3.7854 liters

Ⓐ 41.64 liters

Ⓑ 13.69 liters

Ⓒ 2.90 liters

Ⓓ 49.70 liters

3. Leon wanted to know if the height of the door was greater than the length of the board. How many feet long is the board? Round your answer to the nearest tenth.

1 foot ≈ 0.3048 meter

Ⓐ 1.2 feet   Ⓒ 11.3 feet

Ⓑ 24.6 feet   Ⓓ 13.1 feet

4. Leon converted the measurement for the width of the window from inches to centimeters. What was his correct conversion? Round your answer to the nearest centimeter.

1 centimeter ≈ 0.393 inch

Ⓐ 19 centimeters

Ⓑ 100 centimeters

Ⓒ 122 centimeters

Ⓓ 63 centimeters

Work with a partner.

Talk about your answers to questions 1–4. Tell why you chose the answers you did.

PART TWO: Check Your Understanding

Remember: You use conversion to change a measurement from one unit to another unit.

- ▶ Rewrite conversion problems as division or multiplication equations.
- ▶ Use equivalencies to solve conversion equations.

Solve this problem. As you work, ask yourself, "What operation do I use to solve this conversion problem?"

5. Leon's mother sent him to buy juice. The juice comes in 1-quart bottles. Leon bought 6 bottles. How many liters did he buy? Round your answer to the nearest hundredth.

1 liter ≈ 1.057 quarts

Ⓐ 5.68 liters
Ⓑ 7.06 liters
Ⓒ 4.94 liters
Ⓓ 6.34 liters

Solve another problem. As you work, ask yourself, "How do I use the given equivalency to convert this measurement?"

6. Leon's brother drove him to the store, a roundtrip of 7 miles. How many kilometers was their ride? Round your answer to the nearest tenth.

1 mile ≈ 1.609 kilometers

Ⓐ 4.4 kilometers
Ⓑ 8.6 kilometers
Ⓒ 11.3 kilometers
Ⓓ 5.4 kilometers

**Look at the answer choices for each question.
Read why each answer choice is correct or not correct.**

5. Leon's mother sent him to buy juice. The juice comes in 1-quart bottles. Leon bought 6 bottles. How many liters did he buy? Round your answer to the nearest hundredth.

> 1 liter ≈ 1.057 quarts

● 5.68 liters

This answer is correct because, to convert quarts to liters, you divide 6 quarts by 1.057, to get 5.6764427 liters, which rounds to 5.68 liters.

Ⓑ 7.06 liters

This answer is not correct because, to convert quarts to liters, you divide 6 quarts by 1.057, to get 5.6764427 liters, which rounds to 5.68 liters. Maybe you added 6 and 1.057 and then rounded.

Ⓒ 4.94 liters

This answer is not correct because, to convert quarts to liters, you divide 6 quarts by 1.057, to get 5.6764427 liters, which rounds to 5.68 liters. Maybe you subtracted 1.057 from 6 and then rounded.

Ⓓ 6.34 liters

This answer is not correct because, to convert quarts to liters, you divide 6 quarts by 1.057, to get 5.6764427 liters, which rounds to 5.68 liters. Maybe you multiplied 6 by 1.057 and then rounded.

6. Leon's brother drove him to the store, a roundtrip of 7 miles. How many kilometers was their ride? Round your answer to the nearest tenth.

> 1 mile ≈ 1.609 kilometers

Ⓐ 4.4 kilometers

This answer is not correct because to convert miles to kilometers, you multiply 7 miles by 1.609, to get 11.263, which rounds to 11.3 kilometers. Maybe you divided 7 by 1.609 and then rounded.

Ⓑ 8.6 kilometers

This answer is not correct because to convert miles to kilometers, you multiply 7 miles by 1.609, to get 11.263, which rounds to 11.3 kilometers. Maybe you added 7 and 1.609 and then rounded.

● 11.3 kilometers

This answer is correct because to convert miles to kilometers, you multiply 7 miles by 1.609, to get 11.263, which rounds to 11.3 kilometers.

Ⓓ 5.4 kilometers

This answer is not correct because to convert miles to kilometers, you multiply 7 miles by 1.609, to get 11.263, which rounds to 11.3 kilometers. Maybe you subtracted 1.609 from 7 and then rounded.

Sometimes when you are asked to convert a measurement, you are not given an equivalency. However, you can use conversion facts.

▶ Here are some common conversion facts.

Multiply	by	to get	Divide	by	to get
miles	1.609	kilometers	kilometers	1.609	miles
feet	0.3048	meters	meters	0.3048	feet
centimeters	0.393	inches	inches	0.393	centimeters
liters	1.057	quarts	quarts	1.057	liters
gallons	3.7854	liters	liters	3.7854	gallons
kilograms	2.205	pounds	pounds	2.205	kilograms
grams	0.035	ounces	ounces	0.035	grams

The meteorologist from a local television station visited Leon's class. She told the students some interesting facts about winter weather. Do Numbers 7 through 10.

7. Leon learned that a hailstone that fell in Coffeyville, Kansas, in 1970 weighed 750 grams. What was the hailstone's weight in ounces?
   Ⓐ 26.25 ounces
   Ⓑ 11.40 ounces
   Ⓒ 2,142.86 ounces
   Ⓓ 749.97 ounces

8. The meteorologist told the class that the hailstone that fell in Coffeyville was 44.5 centimeters around its middle. How many inches represent the same measurement? Round your answer to the nearest tenth.
   Ⓐ 48.4 inches
   Ⓑ 17.5 inches
   Ⓒ 44.1 inches
   Ⓓ 11.4 inches

9. On February 6, 1978, a blizzard dropped 26 inches of snow on New York City. How many centimeters represent the same measurement? Round your answer to the nearest centimeter.
   Ⓐ 10 centimeters
   Ⓑ 84 centimeters
   Ⓒ 102 centimeters
   Ⓓ 66 centimeters

10. Leon learned that during the year of 1971–1972, 102 feet of snow fell at Mount Rainier, in Washington. How many meters is 102 feet? Round your answer to the nearest hundredth.
   Ⓐ 334.65 meters
   Ⓑ 102.70 meters
   Ⓒ 31.09 meters
   Ⓓ 10.36 meters

To prepare for the meteorologist's visit, Leon's class had studied weather for several weeks. They did some experiments and some research, and they made a poster to show what they learned. Read their poster. Then do Numbers 11 through 14.

PROJECT RAIN

What is rain? *Rain forms in a cloud when tiny drops of water join together to form larger drops. When these large drops become heavy, they fall to the ground as rain.*

Amazing Rain Facts	Our Rainfall Experiment	Raining Cats and Dogs?
! Tutunendo, Columbia, holds the record for the greatest average annual rainfall. In an average year, Tutunendo gets about 1,178 centimeters of rain. ! The U.S. record for the most rain in 24 hours belongs to Alvin, Texas. From July 25 to July 26, 1979, 48 centimeters of rain fell.	Week 1 3 cm Week 2 1.5 cm Week 3 4 cm Week 4 2 cm **Total Rainwater Collected** 1.5 quarts	*Sometimes, storm winds pick things up and drop them back to earth like rain.* • On June 16, 1939, tiny frogs rained down on Trowbridge, England. The frogs came from nearby ponds and streams. • On February 9, 1859, people in Glamorgan, Wales, were stunned when fish fell from the sky. The fish covered an area almost as large as a football field.

THE RAIN FOREST

In South American rain forests, it rains almost every day.
In one year, a rain forest gets from 2 to 4 meters of rain.

11. Leon learned that Tutunendo has an average yearly rainfall of 1,178 centimeters. How many inches is 1,178 centimeters? Round your answer to the nearest inch.

  Ⓐ 2,998 inches   Ⓒ 785 inches

  Ⓑ   463 inches   Ⓓ 299 inches

12. Leon's class collected rainwater in a bucket and measured it each week. Over 4 weeks, they had collected a total of 1.5 quarts of rainwater. How many liters of water is this? Round your answer to the nearest hundredth.

  Ⓐ 1.42 liters   Ⓒ 2.56 liters

  Ⓑ 1.59 liters   Ⓓ 0.44 liters

13. According to the students' research, a South American rain forest gets 2 to 4 meters of rain each year. What is the equivalent range in feet? Round your answer to the nearest tenth.

  Ⓐ 0.6–1.2 feet   Ⓒ 1.2–5.0 feet

  Ⓑ 5.0–6.6 feet   Ⓓ 6.6–13.1 feet

14. Leon read about the Gulf Stream, an ocean current that affects weather in many places. The Gulf Stream flows through the Atlantic Ocean at a speed of 111 miles a day. How many kilometers is this? Round your answer to the nearest tenth.

  Ⓐ 168.6 kilometers   Ⓒ 69.0 kilometers

  Ⓑ 178.6 kilometers   Ⓓ 67.9 kilometers

▶ A test question about customary and metric measures may require you to use multiplication to convert a measurement from a customary unit to a metric unit, or from a metric unit to a customary unit.

▶ A test question about customary and metric measures may require you to use division to convert a measurement from a customary unit to a metric unit, or from a metric unit to a customary unit.

Leon wrote a report about the state of Pennsylvania. Read this part of his report. Then do Numbers 15 and 16.

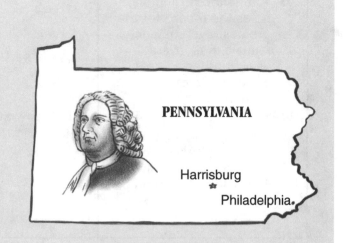

Pennsylvania

Pennsylvania was one of America's original Thirteen Colonies. It was first settled by Swedes in 1634. In 1681, a royal charter for the colony was granted to William Penn by the king of England. Penn decided to name the state in honor of his father, Admiral Sir William Penn. The name Pennsylvania means "Penn's woodland." Pennsylvania became a state on December 12, 1787. It was the second state admitted to the Union. Pennsylvania's capital is Harrisburg, and its largest city is Philadelphia. Philadelphia is an important historical city. It was the capital of the United States from 1776 to 1800. The Declaration of Independence was signed in Philadelphia in 1776, and the Constitution was written there in 1787.

PENNSYLVANIA

Harrisburg

Philadelphia

Converting Customary and Metric Measures

15. Leon learned some interesting facts about Pennsylvania while he was doing research for his report. He found out that the highest point in Pennsylvania is Mount Davis, at 3,213 feet. What is Mount Davis's height in meters? Round your answer to the nearest meter.

Ⓐ   979 meters

Ⓑ 6,261 meters

Ⓒ 10,541 meters

Ⓓ   268 meters

Converting Customary and Metric Measures

16. Leon read about the Liberty Bell, which is kept at Independence Hall in Philadelphia. He learned that the bell weighs 2,080 pounds. What is the bell's weight in kilograms? Round your answer to the nearest tenth.

Ⓐ 4,622.2 kilograms

Ⓑ   497.7 kilograms

Ⓒ   943.3 kilograms

Ⓓ 6,615.0 kilograms

At the end of each school year, Leon's school has a field day. Read about this event. Then do Numbers 17 and 18.

ATTENTION, STUDENTS!

This year's field day will take place on Friday, June 9. There will be a wide variety of fun and challenging games and events. As we have done every year, the students will be divided into two teams—the red team and the blue team. On Thursday, June 8, your teacher will tell you which team you are on. On Friday, please try to wear a shirt in the color of your team.

After attendance is taken on Friday morning, students and teachers are encouraged to participate in the warm-up walk around the school. This is a 1-mile walk that takes 4 trips around the building. Activities will begin at 10:30 A.M., following the walk.

At 11:30, we will take a break for the special field-day barbecue. Principal Jamison and the cafeteria staff will prepare hotdogs and hamburgers for everyone!

After lunch, the activities will continue until 2:15. Then there will be an awards ceremony and ice-cream treats.

Remember to bring a water bottle and to dress appropriately for outside activities. In case of rain, field day will be held on Monday, June 12.

Converting Customary and Metric Measures

17. Leon's class sponsored a "bucket-brigade" race. In this race, each team must line up and pass along cups of water, emptying the cups into a bucket at the end of the line. The winner is the team that fills their bucket first. Each bucket holds 20 liters. How many quarts are equal to 20 liters? Round your answer to the nearest quart.

    Ⓐ 19 quarts   Ⓒ 38 quarts
    Ⓑ 21 quarts   Ⓓ 11 quarts

Converting Customary and Metric Measures

18. Leon also participated in the mini-marathon. This was a 3-kilometer run for students in the fifth and sixth grades. How many miles is 3 kilometers? Round your answer to the nearest tenth.

    Ⓐ 1.9 miles
    Ⓑ 4.6 miles
    Ⓒ 4.8 miles
    Ⓓ 1.4 miles

Strategy Nine USING ALGEBRA

Study Brett's notes about basketball rules and his favorite team. As you study, look for patterns. Also think about how the numbers could be used to write equations.

Rules

A field goal can be made by shooting from anywhere on the court. A shot made from beyond the three-point line is worth 3 points. A shot made inside of the three-point line is worth 2 points. When certain fouls are made, a free throw is taken from the free-throw line. A free throw is worth 1 point.

Statistics for the Chargers

The team scores a 2-point field goal on about 5 out of 8 shots taken.
The team scores a 3-point field goal on about 1 out of 4 shots taken.
The team makes about 3 out of 4 free throws.

In one game, a player made 5 baskets inside of the three-point line and 3 free throws.
You can write and solve an equation to find the total points the player scored.

$(5 \times 2) + (3 \times 1) = \square$ $10 + 3 = \square$ or 13   The player scored a total of 13 points.

The coach of the Chargers expects the team to take about 80 two-point shots in each game.
You can write and solve a proportion to estimate how many of those shots will result in field goals.

$$\frac{5 \text{ field goals}}{8 \text{ shots taken}} = \frac{x \text{ field goals}}{80 \text{ shots taken}}$$

Write the cross products for the proportion.

$8x = 5 \times 80$
$8x = 400$
$x = 400 \div 8$
$x = 50$

The Chargers can expect to score about 50 field goals.

The number of points scored for three-point field goals can be shown in a pattern.
Since each field goal is worth 3 points, the pattern is to multiply the number of field goals by the number of points (3). The next number in the pattern is 15 (5 × 3).

3, 6, 9, 12, ___

You use **algebra** when you write equations and find patterns.

▶ Write and then solve an equation to find the answer to some problems.

▶ Write and then solve a proportion to find the answer to some problems.

▶ Use patterns to find missing numbers.

Brett obtained a scale drawing of a basketball court used by the National Basketball Association. Study the measurements in the drawing. Then do Numbers 1 through 4.

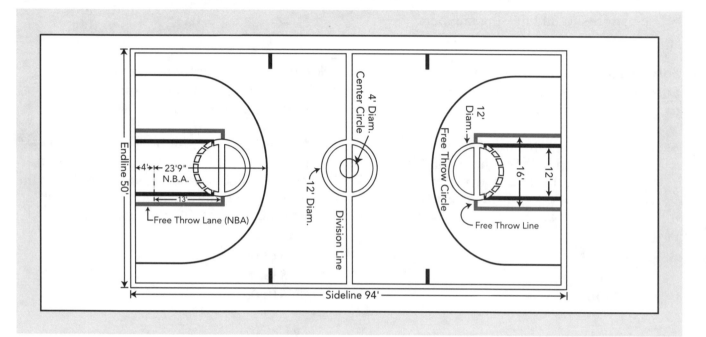

1. The artist used a scale of $\frac{1}{2}$ inch = 10 feet to make the drawing. Using this scale, what would the length of the endline be on the drawing?

   Ⓐ 5 inches
   Ⓑ 10 inches
   Ⓒ $2\frac{1}{2}$ inches
   Ⓓ $2\frac{1}{2}$ feet

2. Brett wants to know what the perimeter of the basketball court is. Which equation would he use to find this information?

   Ⓐ 94' + 50' = ☐
   Ⓑ 4 × 94' = ☐
   Ⓒ (2 × 94') + (2 × 50') = ☐
   Ⓓ 4 × 50' = ☐

3. The missing number in this pattern is the same as the number of points the Chargers scored in their last game. What was the Chargers' score?

   1, 4, 16, ____, 256

   Ⓐ 64 points
   Ⓑ 128 points
   Ⓒ 32 points
   Ⓓ 48 points

4. Brett plans to make his own scale drawing of the basketball court. He will use a scale of $\frac{1}{4}$ inch = 2 feet. What will the diameter of the center circle be on his drawing?

   Ⓐ 2 inches
   Ⓑ $\frac{1}{2}$ inch
   Ⓒ 4 inches
   Ⓓ 8 inches

Talk about your answers to questions 1–4. Tell why you chose the answers you did.

Remember: You use algebra when you write equations and find patterns.

▶ Write and then solve an equation to find the answer to some problems.

▶ Write and then solve a proportion to find the answer to some problems.

▶ Use patterns to find missing numbers.

Solve this problem. As you work, ask yourself, "How can I set up a proportion to solve the problem?"

5. Brett determined that for every 12 days of school, he spends 14.5 hours on math homework. At this rate, how many hours of math homework does he do every 5 days? Express your answer to the nearest hour.

Ⓐ 35 hours

Ⓑ 4 hours

Ⓒ 6 hours

Ⓓ 1 hour

Solve another problem. As you work, ask yourself, "What equation can I use to solve the problem?"

6. Brett bought 3 kits at the hobby store. The total cost of the items before tax was $50. Two of the kits were the same price, and the third was $2 more than the others. What was the price of the more expensive kit?

Ⓐ $16.67

Ⓑ $18.00

Ⓒ $32.00

Ⓓ $10.00

Look at the answer choices for each question.
Read why each answer choice is correct or not correct.

5. Brett determined that for every 12 days of school, he spends 14.5 hours on math homework. At this rate, how many hours of math homework does he do every 5 days? Express your answer to the nearest hour.

Ⓐ 35 hours

This answer is not correct because the proportion to solve the problem is $\frac{12}{14.5} = \frac{5}{x}$, or 12x = 72.5, or x = 6.04, which, to the nearest hour, is 6 hours. Maybe you used the proportion $\frac{12}{x} = \frac{5}{14.5}$.

Ⓑ 4 hours

This answer is not correct because the proportion to solve the problem is $\frac{12}{14.5} = \frac{5}{x}$, or 12x = 72.5, or x = 6.04, which, to the nearest hour, is 6 hours. Maybe you used the proportion $\frac{12}{14.5} = \frac{x}{5}$.

● 6 hours

This answer is correct because the proportion to solve the problem is $\frac{12}{14.5} = \frac{5}{x}$, or 12x = 72.5, or x = 6.04, which, to the nearest hour, is 6 hours.

Ⓓ 1 hour

This answer is not correct because the proportion to solve the problem is $\frac{12}{14.5} = \frac{5}{x}$, or 12x = 72.5, or x = 6.04, which, to the nearest hour, is 6 hours. Maybe you used the proportion $\frac{14.5}{12} = \frac{x}{1}$.

6. Brett bought 3 kits at the hobby store. The total cost of the items before tax was $50. Two of the kits were the same price, and the third was $2 more than the others. What was the price of the more expensive kit?

Ⓐ $16.67

This answer is not correct because it is the price per kit if each kit were the same price. Maybe you used the equation □ + □ + □ = 50.

● $18.00

This answer is correct because the equation to solve for the most expensive kit is □ + □ + (□ + 2) = 50; so each □ = $16, and □ + 2 = $18, the cost of the more expensive kit.

Ⓒ $32.00

This answer is not correct because the equation to solve for the most expensive kit is □ + □ + (□ + 2) = 50. Maybe you solved for the cost of the two less expensive kits together.

Ⓓ $10.00

This answer is not correct because the equation to solve for the most expensive kit is □ + □ + (□ + 2) = 50. Maybe you solved for (3 × □) + (2 × □) = 50.

You use algebra to plot points on a coordinate grid.

▶ The first number in a coordinate pair shows the movement on the horizontal, or x, axis. The second number in a coordinate pair shows the movement on the vertical, or y, axis.

▶ The coordinate pairs for points A and B are shown on the grid.

Brett made this coordinate grid. Study the points on the grid. Then do Numbers 7 through 10.

7. Which point is named by the coordinate pair (2, ⁻1)?
    Ⓐ E
    Ⓑ C
    Ⓒ F
    Ⓓ D

8. Brett wants to draw a rectangle. He will use points $C, E,$ and F for the vertices. Which coordinate pair can Brett use to complete the rectangle?
    Ⓐ (2, 1)
    Ⓑ (⁻2, 1)
    Ⓒ (⁻1, ⁻2)
    Ⓓ (⁻2, ⁻1)

9. Which coordinate pair shows the location of point G?
    Ⓐ (⁻4, ⁻4)
    Ⓑ (⁻3, ⁻4)
    Ⓒ (⁻4, ⁻3)
    Ⓓ (⁻4, 3)

10. Brett wants to draw a parallelogram. He will use points $A, E,$ and G for the vertices. Which coordinate pair can Brett use to complete the parallelogram?
    Ⓐ (3, ⁻1)
    Ⓑ (⁻3, 1)
    Ⓒ (⁻1, ⁻3)
    Ⓓ (⁻3, ⁻1)

**Brett used this coordinate grid to draw different figures. Study the grid.
Then do Numbers 11 through 14.**

11. Brett wants to make a square using points
    L, *M*, and *N*. Which coordinate pair
    provides the point he has to use to
    complete the square?
    - Ⓐ (⁻1, 3)
    - Ⓑ (3, ⁻1)
    - Ⓒ (⁻1, ⁻3)
    - Ⓓ (⁻3, 3)

12. Which coordinate pair shows the location
    of point *O*?
    - Ⓐ (⁻2, ⁻4)
    - Ⓑ (⁻4, ⁻2)
    - Ⓒ (⁻4, 2)
    - Ⓓ (2, ⁻4)

13. Brett will draw a right triangle using
    the points *R* and *S*. Which coordinate
    pair provides the point he can use
    to complete the right triangle?
    - Ⓐ (2, 1)
    - Ⓑ (4, 1)
    - Ⓒ (⁻1, 2)
    - Ⓓ (2, ⁻1)

14. Which point is named by the coordinate
    pair (⁻3, 1)?
    - Ⓐ *P*
    - Ⓑ *M*
    - Ⓒ *N*
    - Ⓓ *Q*

► A test question about algebra may ask for the solution to an equation or proportion.

► A test question about algebra may ask for the missing number in a pattern.

► A test question about algebra may ask for plot points on a coordinate grid.

Read the nutrition information that Brett found on the label of a can of tuna. Then do Numbers 15 and 16.

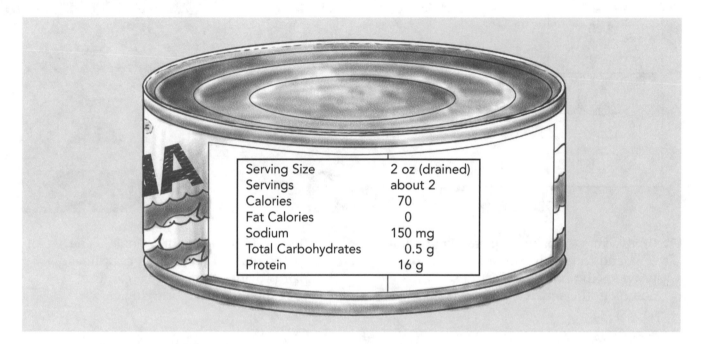

Serving Size	2 oz (drained)
Servings	about 2
Calories	70
Fat Calories	0
Sodium	150 mg
Total Carbohydrates	0.5 g
Protein	16 g

Using Algebra

15. Brett read a recipe for tuna casserole. It calls for 9 ounces of tuna. How many calories are in 9 ounces of tuna?

Ⓐ 180 calories

Ⓑ 630 calories

Ⓒ 315 calories

Ⓓ 35 calories

Using Algebra

16. Brett determined that the missing number in this pattern is the same as the number of mg of cholesterol in half a can of tuna. How many mg of cholesterol are in half a can of tuna?

8, 19, ___, 41, 52

Ⓐ 22 mg

Ⓑ 30 mg

Ⓒ 29 mg

Ⓓ 27 mg

Brett plans to participate in the Bike for Hunger ride. Read the information about the ride. Then do Numbers 17 and 18.

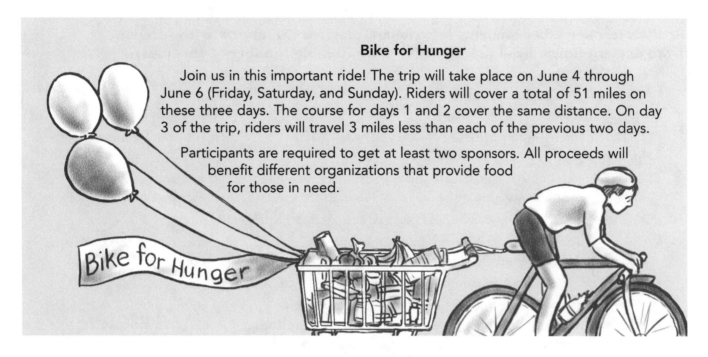

Bike for Hunger

Join us in this important ride! The trip will take place on June 4 through June 6 (Friday, Saturday, and Sunday). Riders will cover a total of 51 miles on these three days. The course for days 1 and 2 cover the same distance. On day 3 of the trip, riders will travel 3 miles less than each of the previous two days.

Participants are required to get at least two sponsors. All proceeds will benefit different organizations that provide food for those in need.

Using Algebra

17. How many miles will the bikers ride on Sunday?

Ⓐ 18 miles

Ⓑ 15 miles

Ⓒ 17 miles

Ⓓ 51 miles

Using Algebra

18. Brett charted the bike trip on this grid. The points show landmarks where he plans to stop. Which coordinate pair shows the location of point *D*?

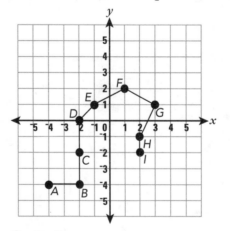

Ⓐ (2, 0)

Ⓑ (0, -2)

Ⓒ (-2, 0)

Ⓓ (-2, 1)

PART ONE: Read an Interview

Rosita's teacher asked students to write an imaginary interview with someone from ancient times. Read Rosita's interview. Then do Numbers 1 through 6.

A construction site in Egypt, 1000 B.C.

ROSITA: Hi, my name is Rosita Ortiz. Can you tell me what you're building here? It looks like the head of a man with a lion's body.

WORKER 1: You are very observant. This is the Sphinx. The head is that of our ruler Pharaoh Khafre. The Sphinx will guard the way that leads to his pyramid, there on the banks of the Nile.

ROSITA: Wow, that pyramid is huge! Is that where Pharaoh Khafre lives?

WORKER 1: A pyramid is not for the living. Pyramids are royal burial places where the bodies of our rulers are placed and protected, after they are mummified, of course.

ROSITA: Can you explain mummification to me?

WORKER 1: I have to get back to work. We're building three Great Pyramids, and we're behind schedule. We haven't quite figured out how we're going to get those $2\frac{1}{2}$-ton stones to the tops of the pyramids. A palace mummifier happens to be here today, over there by the Great Pyramid of Khufu. He can tell you what you want to know about mummies.

ROSITA: Okay, thanks for your time.

ROSITA: Hello, sir. Can you answer some questions about mummies?

WORKER 2: Yes. I am the chief palace mummifier. What do you want to know?

ROSITA: How is a body mummified?

WORKER 2: Well, first we remove the organs, starting with the brain. Then we use a salt compound called *natron* to help the body dry out. That takes about 40 days. Then we embalm the body. After that, we carefully wrap the entire body in cloth bandages. Bandaging alone can take two weeks. Of course, at each stage, we perform sacred rituals that ensure the continuation of the pharaoh's life after death.

ROSITA: Why do you go to so much trouble?

WORKER 2: As I said, we believe life goes on after death, and that the body and the soul are as important to humans in death as they are in life. We also believe that our rulers join the gods in the afterworld. We want to make sure that they find their way, and also that their bodies are still in good shape when they get there.

ROSITA: Thank you for your time. I guess, as you might say, that about *wraps* it up.

Converting Time and Money

1. Rosita built a scale replica of a pyramid 2,000 times smaller than actual size. She spent 48 minutes each day for 4 days, working on her replica. On the fifth day, she spent another $1\frac{1}{5}$ hours. How long did it take Rosita to build the pyramid?
   - Ⓐ 4 hours, 48 minutes
   - Ⓑ 3 hours, 17 minutes
   - Ⓒ 5 hours, 15 minutes
   - Ⓓ 4 hours, 24 minutes

Converting Time and Money

2. Rosita called her aunt, who is a travel agent, and learned that a one-week trip to Egypt to see the Sphinx, the Great Pyramids of Giza, and other sites would cost $1,948. Which of these equals $1,948?
   - Ⓐ 38,960 nickels
   - Ⓑ 487 quarters
   - Ⓒ 19,480 pennies
   - Ⓓ 3,896 dimes

Converting Customary and Metric Measures

3. Rosita read that more than 374 meters of linen could be used to wrap one mummy. What is the linen's length in feet? Round your answer to the nearest foot.

   | 1 meter ≈ 3.2808 feet |

   - Ⓐ 1,342 ft
   - Ⓒ 1,227 ft
   - Ⓑ 13,209 ft
   - Ⓓ 114 ft

Converting Customary and Metric Measures

4. The average weight of each stone used in the Great Pyramids is about 3,000 pounds. What is the weight in kilograms of a 2,943-pound stone? Round your answer to the nearest tenth.

   | 1 pound ≈ 0.45 kilograms |

   - Ⓐ 6,666.7 kg
   - Ⓒ 6,540.0 kg
   - Ⓑ 1,350.0 kg
   - Ⓓ 1,324.4 kg

Using Algebra

5. Rosita charted the inside of the Great Pyramid of Giza. The points show the King's Chamber, Queen's Chamber, Grand Gallery, and other features. Which coordinate pair shows the location of the Grand Gallery, B?
   - Ⓐ $(^-3, 1)$
   - Ⓑ $(^-3, ^-1)$
   - Ⓒ $(^-3, ^-3)$
   - Ⓓ $(3, ^-1)$

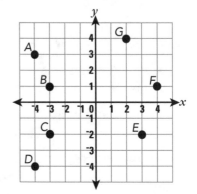

Using Algebra

6. Rosita figured out that the missing number in this pattern is the same as the length in meters of the Great Pyramid's Grand Gallery. How many meters long is the Grand Gallery?

   2, 7, 14, 23, 34, ____ , 62

   - Ⓐ 49 m
   - Ⓒ 36 m
   - Ⓑ 47 m
   - Ⓓ 56 m

Here is the letter that Julie's mom received from Franklin Animal Safari Park. Read the letter. Then do Numbers 7 through 12.

Dear Mrs. Washington:

This letter confirms the receipt of payment in full for the Deluxe Package for 4 at Franklin Animal Safari Park, July 21, 2000.

Your reservation number is **R2498-0812**. You will need this number to obtain your passes when you check in at the park entrance.

Your safari has been scheduled for **10:50 A.M.** If you wish to change this time, please call 555-6837 one week before your scheduled visit.

Here are some points to remember to make your trip to Franklin Animal Safari Park as pleasant and as safe as possible.

- The park is open from 9:30 A.M. to 8:45 P.M., every day except Monday. Your Deluxe Package tickets entitle you to enter the park 90 minutes before regular opening time.

- You may take pictures during your safari ride, but we ask that you do not use the flash on your camera, as the flash disturbs the animals.

- The weather in July in this region can be extremely hot. Wear cool, comfortable clothes. Sunblock and insect repellent are advised.

- Downpours that accompany afternoon thunderstorms are a common event, so you may wish to pack lightweight rain ponchos.

- There are several restaurants situated around the park for your family's dining pleasure. Your Deluxe Package tickets entitle you to a complimentary lunch at the Jungle Flower Café. Please make your reservations for a specific dining time, when you check in at the park.

- Directions: From Route 4, take Exit 27A. Travel approximately $3\frac{1}{4}$ miles on Route 164 West. Take a right onto Safari Road immediately after the giant mechanical giraffe .

We look forward to your visit.

Sincerely,

Your friends at Franklin Animal Safari Park

Converting Time and Money

7. Julie's family arrived at the park $\frac{3}{4}$ hour before it opened to the general public. It takes 73 minutes to drive from their home to the park. At what time did they leave home?

   Ⓐ 8:45 P.M.

   Ⓑ 8:30 A.M.

   Ⓒ 7:32 A.M.

   Ⓓ 7:13 A.M.

Converting Customary and Metric Measures

10. The distance from Julie's house to Franklin Animal Safari Park is 69 miles. How many kilometers is 69 miles? Round your answer to the nearest hundredth.

   | 1 mile ≈ 1.609 kilometers |

   Ⓐ 42.88 kilometers

   Ⓑ 111.02 kilometers

   Ⓒ 117.30 kilometers

   Ⓓ 15.40 kilometers

Converting Time and Money

8. Before leaving home, Julie grabbed a twenty-dollar bill and 2 handfuls of change from her change bank to buy souvenirs. In the car, she counted the coins: she had 27 quarters, 38 dimes, 28 nickels, and 14 pennies. What is the value of these coins?

   Ⓐ $12.09

   Ⓑ $25.01

   Ⓒ $10.11

   Ⓓ $44.19

Using Algebra

11. The day of Julie's visit, the park conducted 16 safaris. Each safari had one jeep containing the safari guide and a park attendant, and 8 other jeeps containing 4 guests each. How many people participated in safaris that day?

   Ⓐ 512 people

   Ⓑ 192 people

   Ⓒ 160 people

   Ⓓ 544 people

Converting Customary and Metric Measures

9. In one day, the Jungle Flower Café served a complimentary lunch with a beverage to 352 people. The beverages served totaled 84 liters. How many quarts are equal to 84 liters? Round your answer to the nearest whole number.

   | 1 liter ≈ 1.057 quarts |

   Ⓐ 89 quarts

   Ⓑ 94 quarts

   Ⓒ 166 quarts

   Ⓓ 75 quarts

Using Algebra

12. Julie used 3 rolls of film to take 66 pictures on the safari. Rolls 1 and 2 had the same number of exposures, and roll 3 had 6 fewer exposures than the other 2 rolls. How many exposures did roll 3 have?

   Ⓐ 24 exposures

   Ⓑ 32 exposures

   Ⓒ 18 exposures

   Ⓓ 12 exposures

PART ONE: Learn About Geometry

Flora visited an art museum. The shapes below show some shapes she saw. As you study, think about the number of sides and angles in the figures.

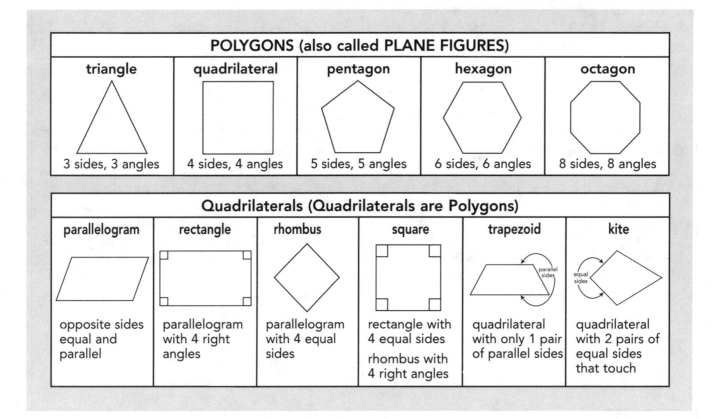

POLYGONS (also called PLANE FIGURES)				
triangle	quadrilateral	pentagon	hexagon	octagon
3 sides, 3 angles	4 sides, 4 angles	5 sides, 5 angles	6 sides, 6 angles	8 sides, 8 angles

Quadrilaterals (Quadrilaterals are Polygons)					
parallelogram	rectangle	rhombus	square	trapezoid	kite
opposite sides equal and parallel	parallelogram with 4 right angles	parallelogram with 4 equal sides	rectangle with 4 equal sides / rhombus with 4 right angles	quadrilateral with only 1 pair of parallel sides	quadrilateral with 2 pairs of equal sides that touch

Circles—A circle is another plane figure. However, a circle is not a polygon, because it does not have straight line segments and angles.

Angle Measures—The sum of the measures of the three inside angles of any triangle is 180°. The sum of the measures of the four inside angles of any quadrilateral is 360°.

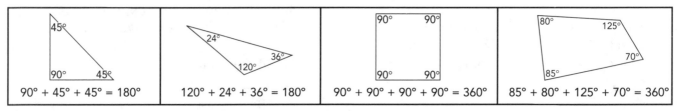

90° + 45° + 45° = 180°	120° + 24° + 36° = 180°	90° + 90° + 90° + 90° = 360°	85° + 80° + 125° + 70° = 360°

You use **geometry** when you work with figures.

▶ Polygons are plane figures named for their number of sides. Quadrilaterals are plane figures described by the length and position of their sides and the size of their angles. Circles are plane figures but are not polygons.

▶ The sum of the measures of the angles of a triangle is 180°. The sum of the measures of the angles of a quadrilateral is 360°.

**Flora helps her parents by taking care of her younger brother.
Look at the puzzle that she and her brother did. Then do Numbers 1 through 4.**

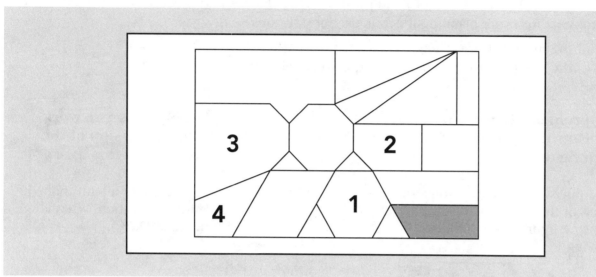

1. Flora told her brother the names of the
   different plane figures in the puzzle. Which
   figure is *not* included in the puzzle?
   Ⓐ hexagon
   Ⓑ triangle
   Ⓒ circle
   Ⓓ pentagon

2. What is the name of the shaded figure
   in the puzzle?
   Ⓐ parallelogram
   Ⓑ trapezoid
   Ⓒ rectangle
   Ⓓ kite

3. Flora knows that two angles in a triangle
   piece have a total measure of 105°. What
   is the measure of the third angle?
   Ⓐ 90°
   Ⓑ 85°
   Ⓒ 75°
   Ⓓ 260°

4. Which numbered figure in the puzzle
   has angle measures that total 360°?
   Ⓐ Figure 1
   Ⓑ Figure 2
   Ⓒ Figure 3
   Ⓓ Figure 4

Work
with a partner.

Talk about your answers to questions 1–4.
Tell why you chose the answers you did.

Remember: You use geometry when you work with figures.

▶ Polygons are plane figures named for their number of sides. Quadrilaterals are plane figures described by the length and position of their sides and the size of their angles. Circles are plane figures but are not polygons.

▶ The sum of the measures of the angles of a triangle is 180°.
The sum of the measures of the angles of a quadrilateral is 360°.

Solve this problem. As you work, ask yourself, "How many sides and angles are in each figure?"

5. Flora's family went on a vacation. This is a drawing of the side view of their hotel. Which plane figure is *not* included in the drawing?

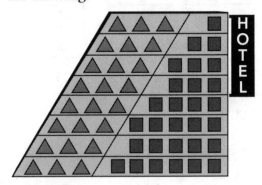

Ⓐ pentagon
Ⓑ triangle
Ⓒ square
Ⓓ parallelogram

Solve another problem. As you work, ask yourself, "What is the sum of the measures of the angles in this figure?"

6. This figure is a diagram of a path that Flora hiked while on vacation. What is the measure of angle *DCB*?

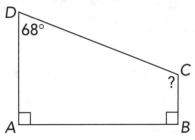

Ⓐ 102°
Ⓑ 90°
Ⓒ 112°
Ⓓ 12°

Look at the answer choices for each question.
Read why each answer choice is correct or not correct.

5. Flora's family went on a vacation. This is a drawing of the side view of their hotel. Which plane figure is *not* included in the drawing?

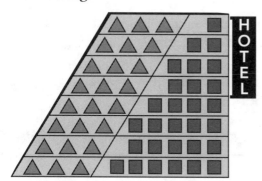

● **pentagon**

This answer is correct because there is no figure in the drawing that has 5 sides and 5 angles.

Ⓑ **triangle**

This answer is not correct because there is a figure in the drawing that has 3 sides and 3 angles.

Ⓒ **square**

This answer is not correct because there is a quadrilateral in the drawing that has 4 equal sides and 4 right angles.

Ⓓ **parallelogram**

This answer is not correct because there is a quadrilateral in the drawing that has opposite sides that are equal and parallel.

6. This figure is a diagram of a path that Flora hiked while on vacation. What is the measure of angle *DCB*?

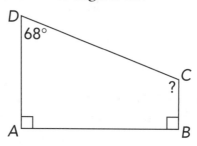

Ⓐ 102°

This answer is not correct because the sum of the measures of the angles of a quadrilateral is 360°, and 90 + 90 + 68 + 102 = 350, not 360.

Ⓑ 90°

This answer is not correct because a right angle measures 90°, and angle ADC is not a right angle.

● 112°

This answer is correct because the sum of the measures of the angles of a quadrilateral is 360°, and 90 + 90 + 68 + 112 = 360.

Ⓓ 12°

This answer is not correct because the sum of the measures of the angles of a quadrilateral is 360°, and 90 + 90 + 68 + 12 = 260, not 360.

You use geometry to measure figures and find measurements.

▶ Perimeter is the distance around a figure. To find the perimeter, add the lengths of all sides.

▶ Circumference is the distance around a circle. To find circumference, use the formula $C = \pi d$. Use 3.14 for π.

▶ Area is the amount of space a plane figure takes up. To find the area of a rectangle, use the formula $A = lw$. To find the area of a triangle, use $A = \frac{1}{2}bh$.

▶ Volume is the amount of space a solid figure takes up. The volume of a cylinder is the area of its base times the height. To find the volume of a cylinder, use the formula $V = \pi r^2 h$.

Flora and her brother Emilio made a special meal for their parents. Study the diagram of the table they set. Then do Numbers 7 through 10.

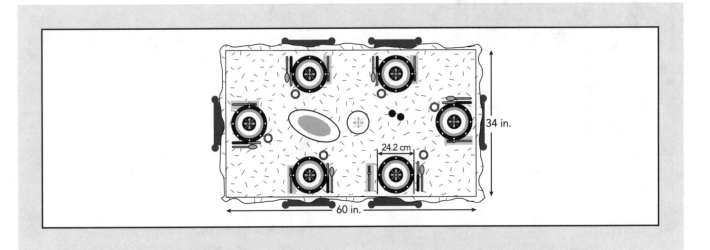

7. Emilio decorated the table by placing a skirt around all of its edges. What was the total length of the skirt needed for the table?
   - Ⓐ   94 in.
   - Ⓑ   120 in.
   - Ⓒ 2,040 in.
   - Ⓓ   188 in.

8. Flora measured the diameter of the plates on the table. The measurement is included in the diagram. What is the circumference of one of the plates?
   - Ⓐ   27.34 cm
   - Ⓑ   75.988 cm
   - Ⓒ 459.7274 cm
   - Ⓓ 106.76 cm

9. Flora calculated the area of the table. What was her correct calculation?
   - Ⓐ 1,452 in.²   Ⓒ 188 in.²
   - Ⓑ 2,040 in.²   Ⓓ   94 in.²

10. Flora wanted to know how much water the drinking glasses hold. What is the volume of this glass?

   - Ⓐ 42.39 in.³   Ⓒ 18 in.³
   - Ⓑ 54 in.³   Ⓓ 13.5 in.³

Flora's town is planning to build a new park. Read part of a proposal that town officials received. Then do Numbers 11 through 14.

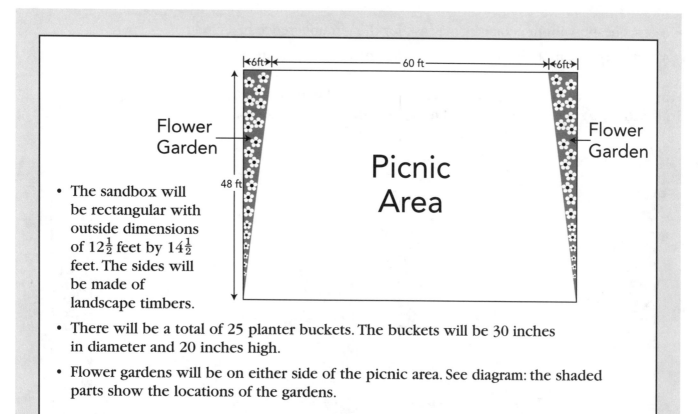

- The sandbox will be rectangular with outside dimensions of $12\frac{1}{2}$ feet by $14\frac{1}{2}$ feet. The sides will be made of landscape timbers.

- There will be a total of 25 planter buckets. The buckets will be 30 inches in diameter and 20 inches high.

- Flower gardens will be on either side of the picnic area. See diagram: the shaded parts show the locations of the gardens.

11. What is the volume of a planter bucket?
Ⓐ   1,884 in.³
Ⓑ   600 in.³
Ⓒ   942 in.³
Ⓓ 14,130 in.³

12. According to the diagram, what is the total area of both flower gardens?
Ⓐ   360 ft²
Ⓑ   288 ft²
Ⓒ 3,456 ft²
Ⓓ   144 ft²

13. Each bucket will have a strip of metal around it, at the top edge. What length does the metal strip need to be?
Ⓐ   94.2 in.
Ⓑ   62.8 in.
Ⓒ 600 in.²
Ⓓ 706.5 in.

14. What is the total length of landscape timbers needed to construct the sandbox?
Ⓐ   27 ft
Ⓑ 181.25 ft²
Ⓒ   54 ft
Ⓓ   25 ft

▶ A test question about geometry may ask for the name of a plane figure.

▶ A test question about geometry may ask for the measure of an angle in a triangle or quadrilateral.

▶ A test question about geometry may ask for the circumference of a circle.

▶ A test question about geometry may ask for the area of a figure.

Flora's dad is building a conference room for a local company. Study the diagram of the room. Then do Numbers 15 and 16.

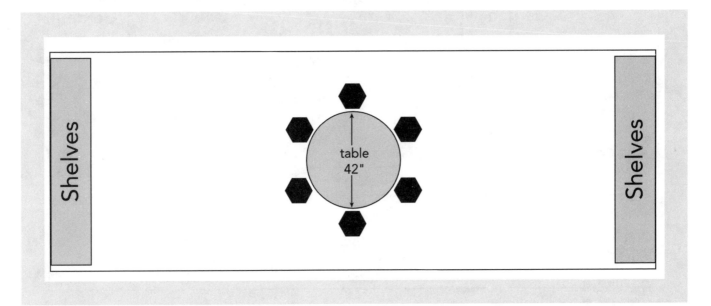

Using Geometry

15. Flora named all of the figures she could see in the diagram. What figure is *not* included?
 Ⓐ rectangle
 Ⓑ circle
 Ⓒ pentagon
 Ⓓ hexagon

Using Geometry

16. To show where the circular table would be placed on the floor, Flora's dad used a rope to show its circumference. What is the total length of rope he needed to do this?
 Ⓐ   42 in.
 Ⓑ   131.88 in.
 Ⓒ 1,384.74 in.²
 Ⓓ   45.14 in.

Flora's aunt owns a restaurant. Study the diagram of the restaurant. Then do Numbers 17 and 18.

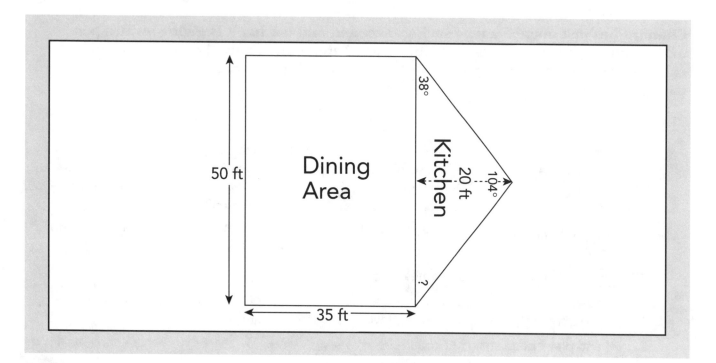

Using Geometry

17. The diagram shows the measure of two angles in the kitchen. What is the measure of the third angle?

   Ⓐ   38°

   Ⓑ   32°

   Ⓒ   90°

   Ⓓ   218°

Using Geometry

18. Flora's aunt is replacing the floor in her kitchen, so she needs to calculate the area of the floor. What is the area?

   Ⓐ   1,750 ft²

   Ⓑ   1,000 ft²

   Ⓒ   700 ft²

   Ⓓ   500 ft²

Strategy Eleven DETERMINING PROBABILITY AND AVERAGES

PART ONE: Learn About Probability and Averages

Chandra has just opened a new savings account, and the bank is giving away a pen to each customer who opens an account. Read about and study the numbers and colors of pens being given away. Think about Chandra's chances of choosing a particular color.

The Midtown Savings Bank gives away a pen to each customer who opens a new savings account. Allison reaches into the box to pick out her pen. The box contains 12 red pens, 18 green pens, 24 blue pens, 10 black pens, and 8 purple pens. Allison wonders, if she picks a pen at random, what her chances are of getting a red or a black pen?

To find the probability that a certain event will happen, find the total number of possible outcomes. Allison has to add the number of pens to find the total number of outcomes.

12 + 18 + 24 + 10 + 8 = 72 outcomes

Next, compare the number of favorable outcomes to the total outcomes. A favorable outcome is the one you are looking for. For Allison, favorable outcomes are red and black pens.

22 red and black pens out of 72 total pens = $\frac{22}{72} = \frac{11}{36}$.

Probabilities can be written as percents. Since a fraction tells you to divide, you can divide the numerator by the denominator to write a decimal. Then multiply the decimal by 100 to find the percent.

$\frac{11}{36}$ = 11 ÷ 36 = 0.30$\overline{5}$, which, to the nearest hundredth, is 0.31.

0.31 × 100 = 31%

Answer: The probability that Allison will get a red or black pen is 11 out of 36, or $\frac{11}{36}$, or about 31%.

You can use facts about known events to make predictions. Allison opened her account with $100. At the end of week 1, she deposited $50. In week 2, Allison withdrew $20. At the end of week 3, she deposited $50. Allison withdrew $20 in week 4. Based on this pattern, how much would Allison have in her account at the end of week 5?

Start	Week 1	Week 2	Week 3	Week 4	Week 5
$100	+ $50	− $20	+ $50	− $20	+ $50

The pattern is to deposit $50 and then withdraw $20.

Answer: At the end of week 5, Allison would have $210 in her account.

You use **probability** to find what the chance is that something will happen.

▶ The probability that a certain event will happen is found by comparing the number of favorable outcomes to the total number of outcomes.

▶ Facts about known events can be used to make predictions.

The baseball league that Allison plays for had a raffle. Read the prize information. Then do Numbers 1 through 4.

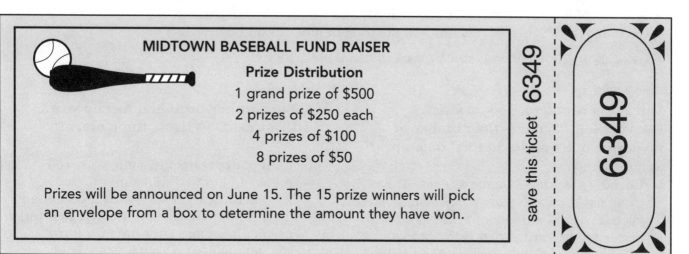

MIDTOWN BASEBALL FUND RAISER

Prize Distribution

1 grand prize of $500
2 prizes of $250 each
4 prizes of $100
8 prizes of $50

Prizes will be announced on June 15. The 15 prize winners will pick an envelope from a box to determine the amount they have won.

save this ticket 6349

6349

1. What is the probability that the first winner to pick from the box wins $250 or more?
   Ⓐ 2 out of 15
   Ⓑ 1 out of 5
   Ⓒ 1 out of 3
   Ⓓ 1 out of 15

2. Allison sold a winning ticket to her aunt. If her aunt picks first, what is the probability that she will win $100 or less?
   Ⓐ $\frac{4}{15}$
   Ⓑ $\frac{8}{15}$
   Ⓒ $\frac{4}{5}$
   Ⓓ $\frac{1}{4}$

3. On Monday, 20 raffle tickets were sold. On Tuesday, 22 were sold. On Wednesday, 20 raffle tickets were sold, and on Thursday, 22 were sold. Based on this data, predict the total number of tickets that will have been sold by Friday night.
   Ⓐ 20 tickets
   Ⓑ 22 tickets
   Ⓒ 84 tickets
   Ⓓ 104 tickets

4. Allison's neighbor bought 25 raffle tickets. If a total of 250 tickets are sold in all, what is the probability that the neighbor will win a prize?
   Ⓐ 10%
   Ⓑ 25%
   Ⓒ   1%
   Ⓓ 100%

Work with a partner.

Talk about your answers to questions 1-4. Tell why you chose the answers you did.

PART TWO: Check Your Understanding

Remember: You use probability to find what the chance is that something will happen.

- The probability that a certain event will happen is found by comparing the number of favorable outcomes to the total number of outcomes.
- Facts about known events can be used to make predictions.

Solve this problem. As you work, ask yourself, "What is the number of favorable outcomes and total outcomes?"

5. Chandra got a board game as a gift. The game has the cards shown below. If a player chooses a card at random from a shuffled pile of all the cards, what is the probability of winning 2 or more points?

Win 1 Point—15 cards
Win 2 Points—10 cards
Win 5 Points—5 cards
Lose 1 Point—10 cards
Lose 3 Points—10 cards

Ⓐ $\frac{1}{4}$
Ⓑ $\frac{1}{5}$
Ⓒ $\frac{3}{10}$
Ⓓ $\frac{1}{2}$

Solve another problem. As you work, ask yourself, "What is the pattern?"

6. Each player starts the game with 100 points. In her first four turns, Chandra wins 2 points, loses 3 points, wins 2 points, and loses 3 points. Based on the first four turns, predict her score after the fifth turn.

Ⓐ 100 points
Ⓑ 0 points
Ⓒ 105 points
Ⓓ 5 points

Look at the answer choices for each question.
Read why each answer choice is correct or not correct.

5. Chandra got a board game as a gift. The game has the cards shown below. If a player chooses a card at random from a shuffled pile of all the cards, what is the probability of winning 2 or more points?

 Win 1 Point—15 cards
 Win 2 Points—10 cards
 Win 5 Points—5 cards
 Lose 1 Point—10 cards
 Lose 3 Points—10 cards

Ⓐ $\frac{1}{4}$

This answer is not correct because the favorable outcomes are Win 2 Points and Win 5 Points. There are 15 cards with these outcomes. The total number of outcomes is 50, and $\frac{15}{50} = \frac{3}{10}$, not $\frac{1}{4}$.

Ⓑ $\frac{1}{5}$

This answer is not correct because the favorable outcomes are Win 2 Points and Win 5 Points. There are 15 cards with these outcomes. The total number of outcomes is 50, and $\frac{15}{50} = \frac{3}{10}$, not $\frac{1}{5}$.

● $\frac{3}{10}$

This answer is correct because there are 15 cards out of a total of 50 that are worth 2 or more points, and $\frac{15}{50} = \frac{3}{10}$.

Ⓓ $\frac{1}{2}$

This answer is not correct because the favorable outcomes are Win 2 Points and Win 5 Points. There are 15 cards with these outcomes. The total number of outcomes is 50, and $\frac{15}{50} = \frac{3}{10}$, not $\frac{1}{2}$.

6. Each player starts the game with 100 points. In her first four turns, Chandra wins 2 points, loses 3 points, wins 2 points, and loses 3 points. Based on the first four turns, predict her score after the fifth turn.

● 100 points

This answer is correct because the pattern is + 2 points then - 3 points; and 100 + 2 - 3 + 2 - 3 + 2 = 100 after the fifth turn.

Ⓑ 0 points

This answer is not correct because the pattern is + 2 points then - 3 points; and 100 + 2 - 3 + 2 - 3 + 2 = 100 after the fifth turn. Maybe you did not start with the 100 points.

Ⓒ 105 points

This answer is not correct because the pattern is + 2 points then - 3 points, which produces a total of 100. Maybe you used the pattern + 3 points then - 2 points.

Ⓓ 5 points

This answer is not correct because the pattern is + 2 points then - 3 points; and 100 + 2 - 3 + 2 - 3 + 2 = 100 after the fifth turn. Maybe you added 2 points + 3 points.

You use what you know about **probability and averages** to find averages and total possible combinations of items.

▶ To find the average, add the items in each group. Then divide the sum by the number of groups. (For the numbers 100, 120, 110, and 70, the sum is 400, and $400 \div 4 = 100$, the average of 100, 120, 110, and 70.)

▶ In some problems, you are given the total. To find the average, you simply divide. (If an orange has 60 calories, then the average number of calories in 1 of 4 equal parts of the orange is $60 \div 4$, or 15.)

▶ To find the total number of possible combinations of items, multiply the number of items by the number of choices. (A shirt is available in short sleeves and long sleeves and in 5 different colors. Multiply the number of styles (2) by the number of colors (5), to find that there are 10 possible combinations.)

Chandra is planning to go to a concert. Do Numbers 7 through 10.

7. There are four different ticket prices for the concert. Concert-goers can buy tickets for $18.50, $21.50, $27.50, or $32.50. What is the average ticket price?
   Ⓐ $100.00
   Ⓑ $ 25.50
   Ⓒ $ 14.00
   Ⓓ $ 25.00

8. The director of the lighting crew at the concert knows that there are 8 different colors of lights and 4 different shapes. How many possible combinations are there of color and shape?
   Ⓐ 12 possible combinations
   Ⓑ 32 possible combinations
   Ⓒ 24 possible combinations
   Ⓓ 36 possible combinations

9. There were 5 performances of the concert. This chart shows the attendance on each night. What was the average attendance at the concert?

Performance	1	2	3	4	5
Attendance	2,389	2,420	2,408	2,415	2,418

   Ⓐ 12,050 people
   Ⓑ 2,415 people
   Ⓒ 2,400 people
   Ⓓ 2,410 people

10. The lead guitarist for one of the bands is trying to decide which guitar and strap to use for one performance. She has 4 different guitars and 5 different straps. How many combinations of guitars and straps are possible?
   Ⓐ 20 possible combinations
   Ⓑ 9 possible combinations
   Ⓒ 10 possible combinations
   Ⓓ 24 possible combinations

Chandra's parents own an appliance store. Study the store's sales chart for dishwashers. Then do Numbers 11 through 14.

A. P. APPLIANCE STORE			
Month	Number of Dishwashers Sold	Month	Number of Dishwashers Sold
January	18	July	19
February	9	August	17
March	21	September	8
April	15	October	12
May	16	November	20
June	15	December	22

11. What is the average number of dishwashers sold each month?

Ⓐ 15 dishwashers

Ⓑ 16 dishwashers

Ⓒ 16.5 dishwashers

Ⓓ 14 dishwashers

12. One stove model at the store is available in 4 different colors. The glass for the stove comes in 3 different colors. How many combinations of stove and glass colors are possible?

Ⓐ 18 possible combinations

Ⓑ 16 possible combinations

Ⓒ 12 possible combinations

Ⓓ 7 possible combinations

13. Brand X makes 5 different refrigerators. A.P. Appliance sells the refrigerators at the prices shown below. What is the average price of a Brand X refrigerator?

Model A—$ 759.00
Model B—$ 829.00
Model C—$ 949.00
Model D—$1,099.00
Model E —$1,139.00

Ⓐ $945.00

Ⓑ $950.00

Ⓒ $949.00

Ⓓ $955.00

14. A customer at the store wants to buy an electric can opener and a blender. The store sells 6 different blenders and 5 different can openers. How many combinations of blenders and can openers are possible?

Ⓐ 28 possible combinations

Ⓑ 30 possible combinations

Ⓒ 24 possible combinations

Ⓓ 11 possible combinations

▶ A test question about probability may ask for the chance that a certain event will happen.

▶ A test question about averages may ask for the average of a group of numbers.

▶ A test question about probability may require you to use facts about known events to make predictions.

▶ A test question about probability may ask you to find a total number of possible combinations.

Chandra made a chart of her family's electric bills. Study the chart. Then do Numbers 15 and 16.

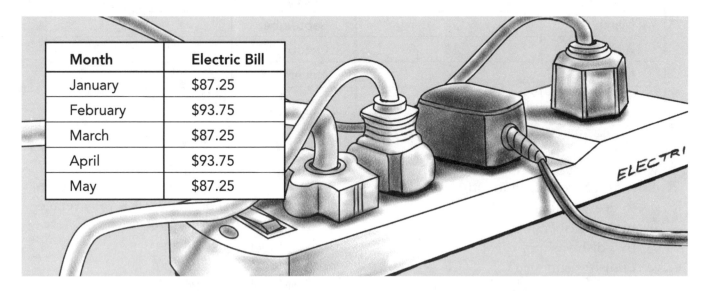

Month	Electric Bill
January	$87.25
February	$93.75
March	$87.25
April	$93.75
May	$87.25

Determining Probability and Averages

15. Based on the information in the chart, predict the total amount paid for electricity in the 6-month period from January to June.
   Ⓐ $543.00
   Ⓑ $449.25
   Ⓒ $536.50
   Ⓓ $ 93.75

Determining Probability and Averages

16. The electric company sells an energy-efficient lamp. The lamp is available in a desktop, floor, or clip-on model. Customers can choose from 8 different colors. How many combinations of style and color are possible?
   Ⓐ 11 possible combinations
   Ⓑ 16 possible combinations
   Ⓒ 24 possible combinations
   Ⓓ 32 possible combinations

Chandra attended an in-line roller-hockey skills competition with her brother. Study the competition rules. Then do Numbers 17 and 18.

Shooting Skills

1. Accuracy: Contestants try to hit a round target placed in the net. Each person gets 10 shots at 60 feet from the goal and 10 shots at 40 feet from the goal. The winner is the contestant with the most combined hits on the target.

2. Speed: Players get 5 shots on net, and the speed of each shot will be recorded. The winner is the player with the highest average speed.

Determining Probability and Averages

17. Chandra's brother knows that he can hit the target with 40% accuracy from 60 feet and with 50% accuracy from 40 feet. How many hits can he expect in the competition?

    Ⓐ 15 hits

    Ⓑ 11 hits

    Ⓒ 9 hits

    Ⓓ 10 hits

Determining Probability and Averages

18. Chandra's speeds in the competition were recorded as 65 mph, 42 mph, 53 mph, 62 mph, and 57 mph. What was her average speed?

    Ⓐ 279 mph

    Ⓑ 57.8 mph

    Ⓒ 58 mph

    Ⓓ 55.8 mph

Strategy Twelve: INTERPRETING GRAPHS AND CHARTS

PART ONE: Learn About Graphs and Charts

Yang has collected sample data about the birthplaces of students in his school, and has calculated the percent of the student sample who were born in a country other than the United States. Study the chart and graph. As you study, think about the number of boys and girls born in different regions.

STUDENTS' BIRTHPLACES					
	United States	Latin America	Europe	Far East	Middle East
Girls	46	18	5	10	5
Boys	52	12	3	8	5

You can use a double-bar graph to show and compare the information in the chart.

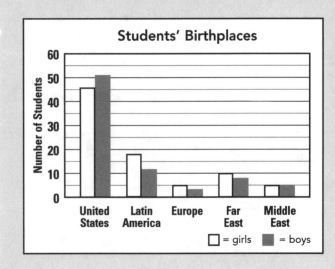

The key shows that the white bar represents boys and the grey bar represents girls. Since there are a total of 164 students in the sample, and 66 of those students were born in a country other than the United States, then $\frac{66}{164}$, or approximately 40%, were born in a country other than the United States.

You use **graphs and charts** to show information about a subject.

▶ A chart uses numbers to show how many.

▶ A bar graph uses bars and numbers to show how many.

Yang and his friend Ben play lacrosse. Think about the numbers that the chart and graph show for goals scored and minutes played by Yang and Ben in the first six games. Then do Numbers 1 through 4.

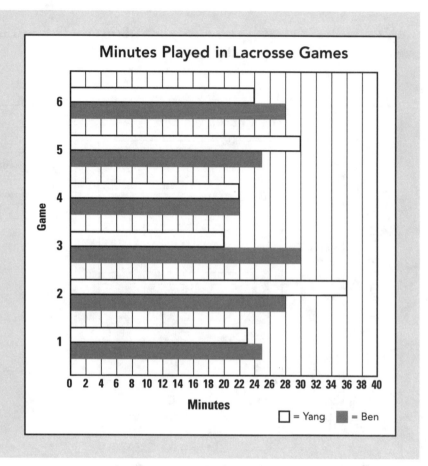

YANG'S LACROSSE TEAM SCORES		
Game	Goals Scored by Yang's Team	Goals Scored by Opponents
1	4	2
2	3	1
3	2	5
4	3	3
5	6	1
6	5	6

Minutes Played in Lacrosse Games

□ = Yang   ■ = Ben

1. What is the total number of minutes that Yang played in the first six games?
   Ⓐ 158 minutes
   Ⓑ 24 minutes
   Ⓒ 145 minutes
   Ⓓ 155 minutes

2. In the first six games, how many more goals did Yang's team score than their opponents?
   Ⓐ 23 more goals
   Ⓑ 5 more goals
   Ⓒ 18 more goals
   Ⓓ 3 more goals

3. How many more goals did Yang's team score in games four through six than in the first three games?
   Ⓐ 5 more goals
   Ⓑ 14 more goals
   Ⓒ 9 more goals
   Ⓓ 2 more goals

4. How many minutes did Ben play in all in the first three games?
   Ⓐ 79 minutes
   Ⓑ 83 minutes
   Ⓒ 158 minutes
   Ⓓ 4 minutes

Work with a partner.

Talk about your answers to questions 1–4. Tell why you chose the answers you did.

Remember: You use graphs and charts to show information about a subject.

▶ A chart uses numbers to show how many.

▶ A bar graph uses bars and numbers to show how many.

Yang's and Ben's classes collected data about their families. The results are shown in the graph and chart.

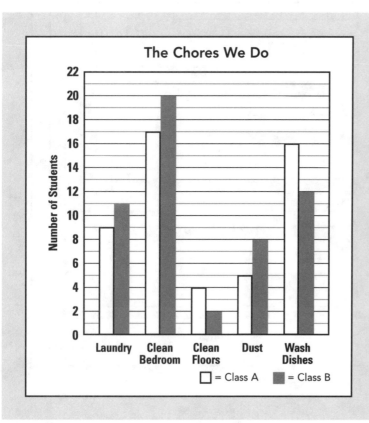

NUMBER OF PEOPLE IN OUR FAMILIES	
Number in Family	Number of Students
2	2
3	6
4	18
5	15
6	6
7	2
8	1

Solve this problem. As you work, ask yourself, "Which bars do I use? What operations do I use?"

5. How many more students in all have to clean bedrooms than dust?
   Ⓐ 12 more students
   Ⓑ 50 more students
   Ⓒ 24 more students
   Ⓓ 29 more students

Solve this problem. As you work, ask yourself, "What data do I use?"

6. What percent of the students have families of 4 or more people?
   Ⓐ 52%
   Ⓑ 42%
   Ⓒ 48%
   Ⓓ 84%

Look at the answer choices for each question.
Read why each answer choice is correct or not correct.

5. How many more students in all have to clean bedrooms than dust?

   Ⓐ 12 more students

   This answer is not correct because 17 + 20, or 37 students have to clean bedrooms and 5 + 8, or 13 students have to dust; and 37 - 13 = 24, not 12.

   Ⓑ 50 more students

   This answer is not correct because 17 + 20, or 37 students have to clean bedrooms and 5 + 8, or 13 students have to dust; and 37 - 13 = 24, not 50.

   ● 24 more students

   This answer is correct because 17 + 20, or 37 students have to clean bedrooms and 5 + 8, or 13 students have to dust; and 37 - 13 = 24.

   Ⓓ 29 more students

   This answer is not correct because 17 + 20, or 37 students have to clean bedrooms and 5 + 8, or 13 students have to dust; and 37 - 13 = 24, not 29.

6. What percent of the students have families of 4 or more people?

   Ⓐ 52%

   This answer is not correct because 18 + 15 + 6 + 2 + 1, or 42 students have 4 or more people in their family. There are 50 students in all, and $\frac{42}{50}$ = 84%. The answer 52% shows the number of students who have 4 or fewer people in their family ($\frac{26}{50}$ = 52%).

   Ⓑ 42%

   This answer is not correct because 18 + 15 + 6 + 2 + 1, or 42 students have 4 or more people in their family. There are 50 students in all, and $\frac{42}{50}$ = 84%. You probably forgot to divide 42 by 50 to find the percent.

   Ⓒ 48%

   This answer is not correct because 18 + 15 + 6 + 2 + 1, or 42 students have 4 or more people in their family. There are 50 students in all, and $\frac{42}{50}$ = 84%. The answer 48% excludes the number of students with just 4 people in their family.

   ● 84%

   This answer is correct because 18 + 15 + 6 + 2 + 1, or 42 students have 4 or more people in their family. There are 50 students in all, and $\frac{42}{50}$ = 84%.

You use graphs and charts to organize information.

▶ Line graphs show changes in amounts over a period of time.

▶ Circle graphs show how each part of a group relates to the whole. The parts of the circle can be identified by fractions or percents. The sum of the percents in a circle graph must equal 100%. The sum of the fractions in a circle graph must equal 1.

Yang, who hopes to study medicine someday, knows that modern medicine has helped us live longer. Study the life expectancy graph. Then do Numbers 7 through 10.

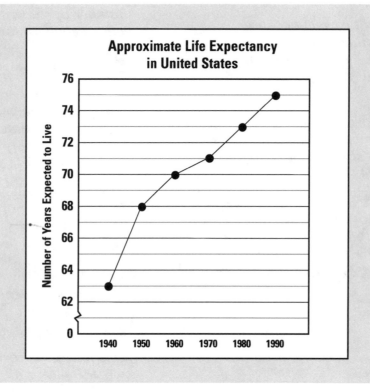

Approximate Life Expectancy in United States

7. During which 10-year period did life expectancy increase the most?
   - Ⓐ 1950–1960
   - Ⓒ 1940–1950
   - Ⓑ 1970–1980
   - Ⓓ 1980–1990

8. During which 10-year period did life expectancy increase the least?
   - Ⓐ 1940–1950
   - Ⓑ 1950–1960
   - Ⓒ 1960–1970
   - Ⓓ 1970–1980

9. What was the difference in life expectancy for 1950 and for 1990?
   - Ⓐ 8 years
   - Ⓒ 12 years
   - Ⓑ 7 years
   - Ⓓ 6 years

10. How much did life expectancy increase from 1960 to 1980?
   - Ⓐ 20 years
   - Ⓑ almost 3 years
   - Ⓒ 2 years
   - Ⓓ 3 years

At Yang's school, the cafeteria offers several choices for lunch.
Look at the circle graph that shows what lunches students bought today.
Then do Numbers 11 through 14.

11. The part of the graph that represents hotdogs does not have a percentage. What percent belongs in this section of the graph?

Ⓐ 24%

Ⓑ 14%

Ⓒ 34%

Ⓓ 25%

12. Which of these two lunch choices combined were chosen by more than 50% of the students?

Ⓐ pizza and chef's salad

Ⓑ hotdog and chicken filet

Ⓒ pizza and hotdog

Ⓓ vegetarian plate and pizza

13. If 400 students bought lunch today, how many bought chicken filets?

Ⓐ 22 students

Ⓑ 88 students

Ⓒ 66 students

Ⓓ 86 students

14. If 400 students bought lunch today, how many bought chef's salad?

Ⓐ 14 students

Ⓑ 56 students

Ⓒ 42 students

Ⓓ 560 students

▶ A test question about charts may ask for information from a chart.

▶ A test question about graphs may ask for information from a double-bar graph.

▶ A test question about graphs may ask for information from a line graph.

▶ A test question about graphs may ask for information from a circle graph.

Yang's school had a new logo designed. Students voted for their favorite design, and the school store now sells clothing with the new logo. Study the chart and graph. Then do Numbers 15 and 16.

Clothes Available with School Logo (prices include tax)		
	Youth Sizes	Adult Sizes
Baseball Cap	$12.95	$14.95
Shorts	$ 8.95	$ 9.95
T-Shirts	$10.00	$10.00

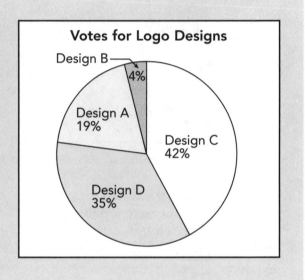

Votes for Logo Designs

Interpreting Graphs and Charts

15. Which group of logo designs received more than 75% of the votes?
   Ⓐ Designs A, B, and D
   Ⓑ Designs A and D
   Ⓒ Designs A and C
   Ⓓ Designs C and D

Interpreting Graphs and Charts

16. Yang bought 2 pairs of youth shorts and 2 adult T-shirts. He paid with 2 twenty-dollar bills. How much change did he receive?
   Ⓐ $ 3.10
   Ⓑ $ 2.10
   Ⓒ $17.90
   Ⓓ $37.90

Yang and his friends enjoy seeing movies at the local theater. Study the graphs that the theater's manager made. Then do Numbers 17 and 18.

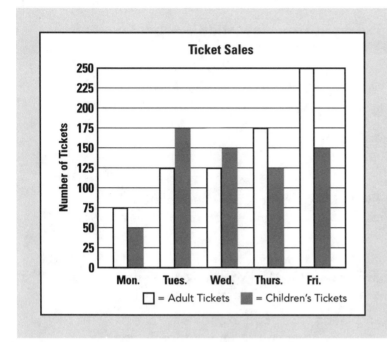

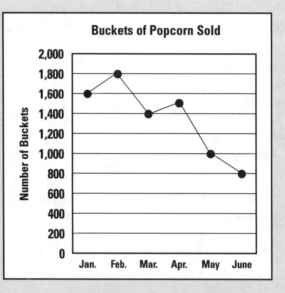

Interpreting Graphs and Charts

17. On which day was there the greatest difference between the number of children's tickets and adult tickets sold?

Ⓐ Tuesday

Ⓑ Wednesday

Ⓒ Thursday

Ⓓ Friday

Interpreting Graphs and Charts

18. What is the difference between the number of buckets of popcorn sold in the months with the greatest and the fewest sales?

Ⓐ 2,000 buckets

Ⓑ 1,000 buckets

Ⓒ 800 buckets

Ⓓ 900 buckets

PART ONE: Read a Memorandum

Here is a memorandum sent to all sixth graders at Longview Middle School. Read the memorandum. Then do Numbers 1 through 6.

MEMORANDUM

To: All Sixth-Grade Students at Longview Middle School
From: The Science Department
Re: Annual Environmental Trip

Each year, the entire sixth-grade class at Longview Middle School is invited to attend a 5-day environmental trip. Although attendance is not mandatory, we do encourage all students to take part in this important learning experience.

The buses will leave on Monday, April 25, at 8:30 A.M. Students will return home on Friday, April 29, at approximately 3:30 P.M. Students will stay at the Wildwood Environmental Center. The fee for the trip includes a room and all meals at the center's dormitory and cafeteria.

During the 5-day trip, students will take part in seminars, perform experiments in the laboratories, and collect plant samples in the center's greenhouses and outdoor study area. The diagram below shows the grounds of the Wildwood Environmental Center.

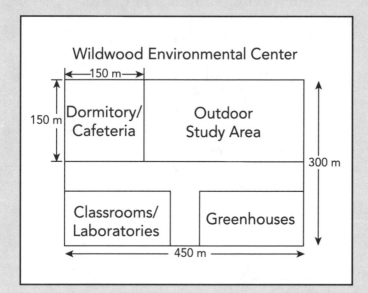

The following is a suggested list of items to take on the trip:

- Boots
- 5 pairs of pants
- Work gloves
- 7 T-shirts (some with short sleeves and some with long sleeves)
- Rain jacket
- Sweatshirts
- Socks and underwear

Throughout the year, we will provide more details about the trip. We will also be involved in fund-raising activities to help lower the cost of the trip. Fees will be calculated after fund-raising has been completed. If there are any questions, please contact the science department.

Using Geometry

1. Look at the diagram in the memorandum. What is the perimeter of the outdoor study area?
   - Ⓐ 45,000 m
   - Ⓑ 1,200 m
   - Ⓒ 900 m
   - Ⓓ 1,100 m

Using Geometry

2. The cafeteria takes up $\frac{1}{4}$ of the space on the first floor of the dormitory/cafeteria building. What is the area of the cafeteria?
   - Ⓐ 22,500 m²
   - Ⓑ 5,625 m²
   - Ⓒ 150 m²
   - Ⓓ 600 m

Determining Probability and Averages

3. Suppose that a student takes the exact number of recommended pairs of pants and T-shirts. How many combinations of pants and shirts would be possible?
   - Ⓐ 35 possible combinations
   - Ⓑ 12 possible combinations
   - Ⓒ 32 possible combinations
   - Ⓓ 2 possible combinations

Determining Probability and Averages

4. Students each get a small tape measure to use during the trip. They are to close their eyes, reach into a bin, and take 1 tape measure. The bin contains 68 silver, 42 red, 26 blue, and 44 yellow tape measures. What is the probability that the first person will pick a red tape measure?
   - Ⓐ $\frac{21}{91}$
   - Ⓒ $\frac{2}{15}$
   - Ⓑ $\frac{11}{45}$
   - Ⓓ $\frac{7}{30}$

Interpreting Graphs and Charts

5. This circle graph shows the types of rocks that some students examined during a seminar. If the students studied a total of 50 rocks, how many were sedimentary?

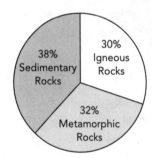

   - Ⓐ 14 rocks
   - Ⓒ 15 rocks
   - Ⓑ 16 rocks
   - Ⓓ 19 rocks

Interpreting Graphs and Charts

6. Students collected parts of plants from the greenhouses and the outdoor study area. This chart shows what one group collected. What percent of the parts were from flowering plants?

Mosses	Ferns	Conifers	Flowering
8	12	4	36

   - Ⓐ 60%
   - Ⓒ 36%
   - Ⓑ 30%
   - Ⓓ 1.7%

This is part of a brochure that describes a new recycling program. Read the brochure. Then do Numbers 7 through 12.

Residents of Longview voted last year to change the town's trash and recycling program. The new trash program is called the "Pay-as-You-Throw" system. Residents purchase special Longview trash bags from local merchants. There are 15-gallon and 30-gallon bags available. These are the only bags that will be picked up by the disposal company.

The goal of this program is to reduce the amount of trash and increase recycling. This graph shows the amount of goods recycled by the average household each month in the past 6 months.

We hope to see these numbers increase in the future.

Here are some suggestions for reducing your disposal costs:

1. Recycle as much as possible.

2. Purchase items that are packaged in recyclable materials, such as paper, most plastics, and glass.

3. Compost yard and vegetable waste.

4. Use the Longview Recycling Center, which is now open from 12:00 P.M. to 7:00 P.M. on Wednesday and Thursday, and from 8:00 A.M. to 8:00 P.M. from Friday through Sunday.

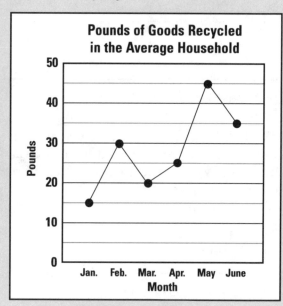

Pounds of Goods Recycled in the Average Household

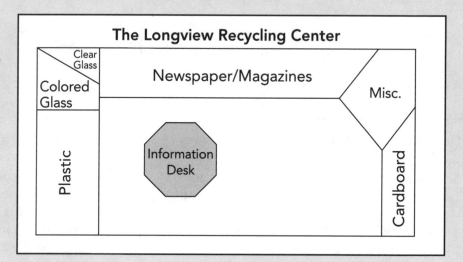

The Longview Recycling Center

Using Geometry

7. Study the diagram of the Longview Recycling Center. Which plane figure is *not* included in the drawing?

  Ⓐ pentagon

  Ⓑ octagon

  Ⓒ hexagon

  Ⓓ quadrilateral

Using Geometry

8. The recycling center has a bin that is shaped like a cylinder. The bin is 48 inches high and has a diameter of 20 inches. What is the volume of the bin?

$$V = \pi r^2 h$$

  Ⓐ   3,014 in.^{3}

  Ⓑ 15,072 in.^{3}

  Ⓒ   960 in.^{3}

  Ⓓ 60,288 in.^{3}

Determining Probability and Averages

9. Residents in one Longview neighborhood collected data about the amount of money spent to buy trash bags during the first year of the program. The 8 households spent the following amounts: $78, $81, $88.50, $75, $99, $54, $81, $85.50. What was the average amount spent for trash bags?

  Ⓐ $80.25

  Ⓑ $82.50

  Ⓒ $81

  Ⓓ $45

Determining Probability and Averages

10. In another neighborhood, $1,932 was spent on trash bags in one year. If there are 21 households in the neighborhood, what was the average yearly cost for one household?

  Ⓐ $98

  Ⓑ $92

  Ⓒ $81

  Ⓓ $82

Interpreting Graphs and Charts

11. According to the line graph, in which month was the amount recycled twice the amount of the previous month?

  Ⓐ February

  Ⓑ March

  Ⓒ April

  Ⓓ May

Interpreting Graphs and Charts

12. This bar graph shows the number of 15- and 30-gallon bags sold at four different locations. How many 30-gallon bags were sold in all at the two locations with the greatest sales for this size?

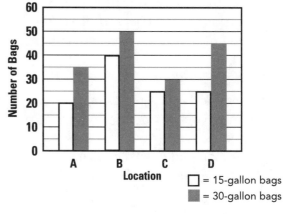

Bags Sold at Each Location Last Week

  Ⓐ 105 bags   Ⓒ   65 bags

  Ⓑ   85 bags   Ⓓ   95 bags

PART ONE: Read an Article

Here is an article that Henry read about marathons. Read the article. Then do Numbers 1 through 12.

Every year, hundreds of thousands of athletes participate in long-distance races known as marathons. Men and women—young and old, on foot and in wheelchairs—compete for prizes, glory, and the sense of accomplishment that comes from completing a race that is approximately 26 miles long.

How Marathons Were Named

Marathons were named for the site of an important battle fought in ancient times between the Greeks and the Persians. After the Greeks defeated the Persians on the plains of Marathon in 499 B.C., the Greek general Miltiades dispatched his swiftest runner, Pheidippides, to proclaim the news of the Greek victory. Pheidippides was not at his best, as he was still recovering from an earlier 150-mile run from Marathon to Sparta to obtain battle support from the Spartans. Nevertheless, he ran the 25 miles to Athens. According to legend, when Pheidippides reached Athens, he gasped out the joyful news of the Greek army's triumph over the Persians and then collapsed. Since then, long-distance runs have been called marathons.

Today's Marathons

The first modern Olympic Games were held in Athens, Greece, in 1896. A 24.8-mile marathon was a major event in that competition and in all the Olympic Summer Games since then.

Marathons are also run each year in such European cities as Vienna, Austria; Venice, Italy; London, England; and Stockholm, Sweden; and in such major American cities as Chicago, Illinois; San Francisco, California; Philadelphia, Pennsylvania; San Antonio, Texas; Taos, New Mexico; Honolulu, Hawaii; and Washington, D.C.

Most people agree that the two most important marathons in the U.S. are those that are held each year in New York City and in Boston. Many marathon enthusiasts consider the historic Boston Marathon to be the most prestigious and the most challenging of the two races. Begun in 1897, the Boston Marathon attracts athletes from around the world. In the 2000 Boston Marathon, more than fifteen thousand people completed the 26.2 mile race. The chart shows the champions of the different divisions of the 2000 Boston Marathon.

DIVISION	NAME	COUNTRY	FINISH TIME
Men's Open	Elijah Lagat	Kenya	2:09:47
Women's Open	Catherine Ndereba	Kenya	2:26:11
Men's Wheelchair	Franz Nietlispach	Switzerland	1:33:32
Women's Wheelchair	Jean Driscoll	United States	2:00:52
Men's Masters	Joshua Kipkemboi	Kenya	2:17:11
Women's Masters	Gitte Karlshoj	Denmark	2:35:11

Building Number Sense

1. In 2000, Boston Marathon prizes, distributed among the winners and runners-up in different divisions, totaled $525,000. Which of these represents the value of the 52 in $525,000?

Ⓐ 5.2×10^4

Ⓑ 5.2×10^7

Ⓒ 5.2×10^8

Ⓓ 5.2×10^5

Applying Subtraction

4. Look at Problem 3. How many more miles did Henry run in week 4 than in week 1?

Ⓐ $10\frac{7}{8}$ mi

Ⓑ $7\frac{3}{4}$ mi

Ⓒ $13\frac{1}{2}$ mi

Ⓓ $10\frac{1}{2}$ mi

Using Estimation

2. Henry read that the average number of spectators along each mile of the 2000 Boston Marathon, rounded to the nearest thousand, was 38,000. He rounded the number of miles to the nearest whole number. About how many spectators gathered along the entire race course?

Ⓐ 988,000 spectators

Ⓑ 1,113,811 spectators

Ⓒ 936,600 spectators

Ⓓ 972,482 spectators

Applying Multiplication

5. Henry learned that of the 16,215 official starters in the 2000 Boston Marathon, approximately 97% finished the race. About how many starters finished the race? Round your answer to the nearest whole number.

Ⓐ 14,215 people

Ⓑ 15,800 people

Ⓒ 486 people

Ⓓ 15,729 people

Applying Addition

3. Henry has been training for 4 weeks to run a half-marathon next fall. The chart shows how many miles he has run each week. How many miles has he run in all?

Week	Miles
1	$21\frac{7}{8}$
2	$24\frac{5}{6}$
3	25
4	$32\frac{3}{4}$

Ⓐ $102\frac{2}{3}$ mi

Ⓑ $104\frac{11}{24}$ mi

Ⓒ $91\frac{15}{16}$ mi

Ⓓ $117\frac{1}{8}$ mi

Applying Division

6. Henry read that approximately 12,500 people had planned to attend the 2000 Boston Marathon pre-race pasta party, at which 11,300 pounds of pasta were served. To the nearest tenth of a pound, how much pasta was there for each person at the party?

Ⓐ 1.0 lb

Ⓑ 0.9 lb

Ⓒ 0.7 lb

Ⓓ 1.1 lb

Converting Time and Money

7. On the morning of the 2000 Boston Marathon, Henry started watching television coverage of the race at the time shown. He watched for $3\frac{3}{4}$ hours, turning the TV off after the winners were presented their awards. What time did Henry stop watching race coverage?

Ⓐ 3:12 P.M.

Ⓑ 1:35 P.M.

Ⓒ 2:28 P.M.

Ⓓ 2:58 P.M.

Using Geometry

10. Henry drew this diagram of the half-marathon course he would run in the fall. What is the measure of the angle *ADC*?

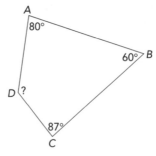

Ⓐ 227°   Ⓒ 133°

Ⓑ 60°   Ⓓ 47°

Converting Customary and Metric Measures

8. Henry learned that the first modern Olympic Games marathon was 24.8 miles. How many kilometers is 24.8 miles? Round your answer to the nearest kilometer.

> 1 mile ≈ 1.609 kilometers

Ⓐ 26 kilometers

Ⓑ 40 kilometers

Ⓒ 15 kilometers

Ⓓ 23 kilometers

Determining Probability and Averages

11. Henry's sister Jan also competed in 5 half-marathons. Her finish times for the 5 races were 87 minutes, 94 minutes, 102 minutes, 89 minutes, and 86 minutes. What was her average time?

Ⓐ 94 minutes

Ⓑ 91.6 minutes

Ⓒ 458 minutes

Ⓓ 89 minutes

Using Algebra

9. Henry's sister Jan ran and won a full marathon. For the first 14 miles, Jan maintained a pace of 0.7 miles every 5 minutes. For the next 12.2 miles, she ran at a rate of 0.8 miles every 5 minutes. To the nearest minute, how long did it take Jan to run the marathon?

Ⓐ 2 hr, 56 min

Ⓑ 3 hr, 25 min

Ⓒ 2 hr, 37 min

Ⓓ 3 hr, 40 min

Interpreting Graphs and Charts

12. Look at the chart in the article. What was the finish time difference between the winner of the Women's Masters Division and the winner of the Women's Open Division?

Ⓐ 35 minutes

Ⓑ 17 minutes

Ⓒ 26 minutes

Ⓓ 9 minutes

Here are two postcards that Seth received from his aunt.
Read the postcard messages. Then do Numbers 13 through 24.

Hi Seth,

Hope all is well with you. Today, I traveled on a train from London to Paris by way of the Channel Tunnel. (Some people call it the "Chunnel.") What an accomplishment this tunnel is! Truly one of the World's Greatest Wonders! The "Chunnel" is 31 miles long and has 3 concrete tubes, each 5 feet thick. A fellow passenger told me that it cost $15 billion dollars to construct, and that it was dug by 13,000 engineers and workers. Trains connecting London to Paris and Brussels travel through 2 of the tubes. I believe that the third tube is used for maintenance and emergency vehicles. We left London at 11:22 P.M. The train zipped along at nearly 100 miles an hour, and "Voila!" (as they say in France), in a mere 2 hours, 58 minutes we were in Paris. Well, I've got to go. I'm going to the Louvre Museum. I'll say "Hi" to the Mona Lisa for you.

Love, Aunt Suzi

Hello Seth,

Europe was marvelous! Did you get all my postcards? I just arrived this morning in São Paulo, Brazil. The weather is beautiful, sunny, and 84°F. I flew here from Asunçion, Paraguay, where I saw another of the World's Great Wonders—the Itaipu Dam. The dam is on the border between Paraguay and Brazil. I hired a taxi for just $50 to take me to the dam and to Iguazu Falls, on the Brazil side of the Paraná River. (I also went to a bird park, which cost $7.86 in American money and ate a wonderful lunch buffet for $12.19.) The Itaipu Dam is the world's largest hydroelectric dam. It's more than 4 miles wide and spans the Paraná River. Someone told me that the dam was built with enough iron and steel to construct 300 Eiffel Towers! It has 18 power plants that generate 12,600 megawatts of power per second. Workers had to shift the course of the Paraná River, the seventh largest river in the world, to construct it. Hope all is well with you. I don't know yet when I'll return. There are still so many wonders of the world that I plan to see, if I can stick to my budget. (Not including the expenses the day I went to Itaipu Dam, my two-day stay in Asunçion cost an additional $179.62 for the hotel and $91.57 for meals.)

Love, Aunt Suzi

Building Number Sense

13. In another postcard that Seth's aunt sent from Brazil, Seth learned that São Paulo produces slightly more than $\frac{3}{5}$ of the country's sugar exports and slightly less than $\frac{7}{20}$ of its coffee exports. What fraction shows the sum of $\frac{3}{5}$ and $\frac{7}{20}$?

Ⓐ $\frac{4}{25}$

Ⓑ $\frac{2}{5}$

Ⓒ $\frac{19}{20}$

Ⓓ $\frac{21}{100}$

Applying Subtraction

16. Seth's aunt saved for 20 years to take her tour of the world's wonders. At the start of her trip, she had $31,384.63 in her savings. By the time she reached São Paulo, Brazil, she had traveled a total of 18,381.72 miles and had used $16,794.78 of her savings. How much money did she have left to continue her travels?

Ⓐ $14,589.85

Ⓑ $ 1,586.94

Ⓒ $13,002.91

Ⓓ $15,610.15

Using Estimation

14. Seth rounded to the nearest dollar each expense his aunt had when she went to the Itaipu Dam, including the trip to the bird park and lunch. What was his correct estimate for her total expenses?

Ⓐ $69

Ⓑ $70

Ⓒ $71

Ⓓ $75

Applying Multiplication

17. From the information in his aunt's postcard message, Seth calculated how many megawatts of power the Itaipu Dam could generate in $8\frac{1}{2}$ seconds. What was his correct solution?

Ⓐ 56,700 MW

Ⓑ 126,000 MW

Ⓒ 107,100 MW

Ⓓ 180,000 MW

Applying Addition

15. Seth added up exactly how much his aunt spent for her two-day stay in Asunçion, including expenses for the day she went to see Itaipu Dam. What was his correct sum?

Ⓐ $296.14

Ⓑ $322.09

Ⓒ $278.29

Ⓓ $341.24

Applying Division

18. Seth figured out how many workers might have worked on the Channel Tunnel at one time if the entire crew of 13,000 were divided into 6 equal groups that rotated shifts. Any personnel left over could pick a group or a shift. How many people were in each group, and how many were left over?

Ⓐ 2,166 R4

Ⓑ 1,299 R2

Ⓒ 2,167 R6

Ⓓ 4,333 R1

Converting Time and Money

19. Seth figured how long it would take the Chunnel train to make the round trip from London to Paris and from Paris to London 3 times. How long would it take the train to make 3 round trips?

Ⓐ 18 hours, 34 minutes

Ⓑ 18 hours, 18 minutes

Ⓒ 17 hours, 48 minutes

Ⓓ 16 hours, 59 minutes

Converting Customary and Metric Measures

20. Seth's aunt said that the Channel Tunnel consists of 3 concrete tubes each 5 feet thick. What is the combined thickness of the 3 tubes in meters? Round your answer to the nearest hundredth of a meter.

> 1 ft ≈ 3.281 meters

Ⓐ 1.52 meters

Ⓑ 49.22 meters

Ⓒ 16.41 meters

Ⓓ 4.57 meters

Using Algebra

21. The missing number in the pattern is the same as the total number of postcards that Aunt Suzi sent Seth during her world travels. How many postcards did she send Seth?

9, 36, ____, 576, 2,304

Ⓐ 45 postcards

Ⓑ 144 postcards

Ⓒ 288 postcards

Ⓓ 136 postcards

Using Geometry

22. Here are some of the more unusually shaped postcards that Aunt Suzi sent Seth. Which figure did Seth correctly determine is *not* included?

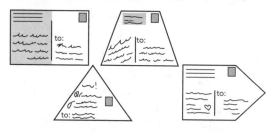

Ⓐ pentagon

Ⓑ triangle

Ⓒ octagon

Ⓓ trapezoid

Determining Probability and Averages

23. For the first 6 months that his aunt was gone, Seth made a chart to track how many postcards she sent. Based on this data, how many postcards did Seth receive from his aunt from April through September?

Month	April	May	June	July	Aug
Postcards	9	8	12	9	8

Ⓐ 46 postcards

Ⓒ 55 postcards

Ⓑ 58 postcards

Ⓓ 54 postcards

Interpreting Graphs and Charts

24. Before her trip, Seth made a graph to show how much time Aunt Suzi would spend in each of the 6 continents she planned to visit. In which continents combined would she spend more than 45% of her time?

Ⓐ A, F

Ⓑ B, D, F

Ⓒ C, E

Ⓓ A, C

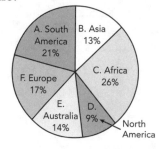

Rick writes a science column for the school newspaper. Here is a column he wrote in which he answered students' questions about the solar system. Read the column. Then do Numbers 25 through 36.

Ask Rick

What does Earth's position in the solar system have to do with life on our planet?

Everything! Earth, as you know, is the third planet from the sun, which turns out to be the perfect location. It's close enough to the sun to be warmed by it, but not so far away to be frozen. Earth's distance from the sun also allows for water to exist on this planet in a liquid state. Water, of course, sustains life—yours and mine, and that of the animals, plants, fish, birds, and insects. Recently, scientists think they have discovered water in its liquid state on Mars. Does that mean that Martians exist or have existed? Not likely, but then again . . . !

I read that in space, all the planets, asteroids, comets, and even the sun are in constant motion. What makes objects in space move around?

Gravity keeps objects in space moving toward each other; it's kind of like a celestial tug-of-war up there. You may have learned that all objects have mass. The greater an object's mass, the greater its gravitational pull on other objects. In our solar system, the object with the greatest mass is the sun. In fact, about 99.85% of the solar system's mass is in the sun. Its gravitational pull on the planets keeps them in orbit. Without the sun, all the planets would go flying off into space. (By the way, the sun's mass is 2.19×10^{27} tons; its volume is 3.387×10^{17} cu mi.)

What exactly is the Milky Way?

The Milky Way is a galaxy of billions of stars, star clusters, planets, and clouds of dust and gas. Our solar system is located on the outside edge of the Milky Way. When you look up at the sky on a clear, summer night, you will see a milky white path of stars stretching across the sky. That's the Milky Way. All the stars in the Milky Way are in a constant spinning motion around the center of the galaxy; they are held there by gravity.

Rick's Starry News: Anyone interested in a set of building plans for a telescope can write to me at the column address. The price for a set of plans is $3.80 plus 5% sales tax and $1.43 for shipping.

One of the best home telescopes you can buy is the Astroview. It costs $2,800.65 in stores. The same telescope can be purchased for $482.99 less on-line, and from the manufacturer for $260 less than the on-line price. Write me for details.

Building Number Sense

25. Rick pointed out that the sun's volume is 3.387×10^{17} cu mi. What is the place value of the 8 in 3.387?

- Ⓐ 80 hundreds
- Ⓑ 8 ones
- Ⓒ 8 tenths
- Ⓓ 8 hundredths

Using Estimation

26. In a previous column, Rick explained that the highest mountain in the solar system is Olympus Mons on Mars. Olympus Mons is 25 kilometers high. Rick converted that figure to $15\frac{27}{50}$ miles and rounded it to the nearest mile for his readers. To the nearest mile, how high is Olympus Mons?

- Ⓐ 16 miles
- Ⓑ 17 miles
- Ⓒ 15 miles
- Ⓓ 20 miles

Applying Addition

27. In last month's column, Rick compared the mass of 4 planets. Using the number 1 to equal Earth's mass, Rick made the chart below. What number is closest to the total mass of the 4 planets in the chart?

Planet	Mass (Earth = 1)
Mercury	0.0553
Venus	0.815
Earth	1
Mars	0.1074

- Ⓐ 1.573
- Ⓑ 1.978
- Ⓒ 1.100
- Ⓓ 2.547

Applying Subtraction

28. Rick gave readers information about buying one of the best home telescopes. How much would the telescope cost if purchased from the manufacturer?

- Ⓐ $2,057.66
- Ⓑ $2,540.65
- Ⓒ $ 742.99
- Ⓓ $2,168.76

Applying Multiplication

29. Rick received 9 orders for telescope plans. How much money should he have received for all 9 orders?

- Ⓐ $47.07
- Ⓑ $35.91
- Ⓒ $49.41
- Ⓓ $48.78

Applying Division

30. By the middle of the school year, Rick had received 268 letters from students who had science questions. Of the 320 questions asked, 210 questions had something to do with the solar system. What percentage of the questions were about the solar system? Round your answer to the nearest percent.

- Ⓐ 65%
- Ⓑ 66%
- Ⓒ 34%
- Ⓓ 44%

Converting Time and Money

31. Rick is saving money that he earns delivering papers and mowing lawns to buy the Astroview telescope. He has saved $1,860. Which of these equals $1,860?

Ⓐ   7,440 quarters

Ⓑ   18,660 pennies

Ⓒ   3,720 nickels

Ⓓ   9,300 dimes

Using Geometry

34. Once, Rick told how to build a scale model of Earth, with a diameter of 11.5 inches. The plans call for string the same length as the circumference of the model. How much string is needed?

$$C \approx \pi d$$

Ⓐ   5.75 in.   Ⓒ   36.11 in.

Ⓑ   415.27 in.²   Ⓓ   72.40 in.

Converting Customary and Metric Measures

32. In a column about space exploration, Rick explained that the U.S. launched the 30-pound *Explorer I* four months after the former Soviet Union launched *Sputnik I* in 1957. What was *Explorer I*'s weight in kilograms?

$$1 \text{ pound} \approx 0.45 \text{ kilogram}$$

Ⓐ   14.0 kg   Ⓒ   30.5 kg

Ⓑ   66.7 kg   Ⓓ   13.5 kg

Determining Probability and Averages

35. In the month following the appearance of a comet in the night sky, Rick received a total of 80 letters, and 64 of them contained a question about the comet. Rick put all 80 letters into a box. What is the probability that the first letter he takes from the box to reread will contain a question about the comet?

Ⓐ 80%   Ⓒ 20%

Ⓑ 64%   Ⓓ 16%

Using Algebra

33. In response to a question about stars, Rick included the following grid to locate major constellations in the Northern Hemisphere. Which coordinate pair shows the location of constellation *L*?

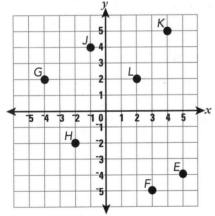

Ⓐ (⁻2, ⁻2)   Ⓒ (2, 2)

Ⓑ (2, ⁻2)   Ⓓ (⁻1, 2)

Interpreting Graphs and Charts

36. To answer a question about the local weather, Rick used this line graph to show the rise and fall of humidity in a 6-day period. What is the difference in humidity between the days with the greatest and the least humidity?

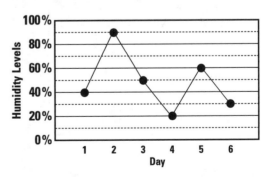

Ⓐ 40%   Ⓒ 70%

Ⓑ 60%   Ⓓ 80%